# Trade and Economic Development in Small Open Economies

# TRADE AND ECONOMIC DEVELOPMENT IN SMALL OPEN ECONOMIES

## The Case of the Caribbean Countries

*Arnold Meredith McIntyre*

Westport, Connecticut
London

**Library of Congress Cataloging-in-Publication Data**

McIntyre, Arnold M.
　Trade and economic development in small open economies : the case
of the Caribbean countries / Arnold Meredith McIntyre.
　　p.　cm.
　Includes bibliographical references and index.
　ISBN 0–275–94745–9 (alk. paper)
　　1. Exports—Caribbean Area.　2. Caribbean Area—Commercial policy.
I. Title.
　HF3312.3.M39　1995
　382'.09729—dc20　　　94–32931

British Library Cataloguing in Publication Data is available.

Library of Congress Catalog Card Number: 94–32931
ISBN: 0–275–94745–9

First published in 1995

Praeger Publishers, 88 Post Road West, Westport, CT 06881
An imprint of Greenwood Publishing Group, Inc.

Printed in the United States of America

The paper used in this book complies with the
Permanent Paper Standard issued by the National
Information Standards Organization (Z39.48–1984).

10 9 8 7 6 5 4 3 2 1

**Copyright Acknowledgments**

The author and publisher gratefully acknowledge permission to reprint the following:

Tables 1.1, 1.2, 1.3, 2.1, and 2.2 have been reprinted from World Bank, *World Tables* (1989–90
edition) (Washington, D.C.: World Bank Publications, 1990).

Tables 3.1 and 3.2 have been reprinted from World Bank, *The Caribbean Common Market Trade
Policies and Regional Integration in the 1990's*, Report No. 8381-CRG (Washington, D.C.: Trade,
Finance and Industry Division, World Bank, 1990).

# Contents

# Figures and Tables

**FIGURES**

**TABLES**

# Acknowledgments

I wish to acknowledge the help of some of the many people who contributed to the completion of this work.

I owe an especially great debt to Professor Gerald K. Helleiner of the University of Toronto for his skillful and patient guidance throughout the many chapter drafts. His extremely high standards will be a constant source of motivation for me. I thank the Institute of Social and Economic Research of the University of the West Indies for giving me a research fellowship. Dr. Delisle Worrell and members of the Research Department of the Central Bank of Barbados provided assistance in many areas and offered useful comments on the early drafts of chapters.

The last stages of the work were carried out during the period that I was a country economist at the Caribbean Development Bank in Barbados. The management of the bank and the director of Economics and Programming, Dr. Keith Worrell, did much to aid the completion of the work.

My wife, Jeannine Giraudy-McIntyre, gave me every possible support including tolerating my long absences from home.

# 1

# Introduction

## 1.1 THE IMPORTANCE OF TRADE

One of the salient features of the early academic research on Caribbean economies is the importance attached to the role of exports in the process of economic development [Lewis (1950), Best and Levitt (1968), and Beckford (1972)]. Lewis argued strongly the case for the rapid industrialization of the British West Indies, citing population growth as the major reason for his argument. In the context of rapid industrialization Lewis saw the export sector as playing a key role. Best and Levitt and Beckford were influenced by the center-periphery model and focused on analyzing the pattern of dependence of the Caribbean economy on the center or industrialized economies. They argued that the dependent relationship between the Caribbean economy and the center had lead to the continued underdevelopment of the Caribbean. Therefore, economic development was contingent upon removing the Caribbean economy's dependence on the center and achieving self-sustaining growth. The policy model suggested included increasing self-reliance or import substitution and, in the context of an economic integration movement, regional import substitution [Brewster and Thomas (1967)].

In the center-periphery model, export specialization was a characteristic of the dependent Caribbean economy. Production was skewed in favor of a few primary products that were exported to the industrialized economies for processing such as sugar, bauxite, and oil. There was no explicit notion in this literature of expanding and diversifying the export base as the means of

| Table 1.1<br>Export/GDP Ratios (Averages) in<br>Selected Caribbean Countries[1] (percentages) | | | |
|---|---|---|---|
| Country | 1968–1990 | 1968–1979 | 1980–1990 |
| Barbados | 68.4[2] | 77.2 | 65.2 |
| Guyana | 59.8 | 54.0 | 68.5 |
| Jamaica | 60.7[3] | 49.8 | 61.1 |
| Trinidad and Tobago | 61.4 | 56.7 | 33.3 |

**Sources:** World Bank (1990a) *World Tables* (1989–1990 edition); and the International Monetary Fund, *International Financial Statistics* (various issues).

**Notes:** [1]Exports of nonfactor services (mainly tourist receipts) are included in total exports in Barbados and Jamaica given the importance of tourism earnings in these countries; [2]The year 1970 is the earliest year for which data on exports of goods and services are available for Barbados; [3]Data on exports of goods and services are only available from 1970 for Jamaica.

increasing the pace of economic growth and development. In other words, the development model that was advocated was "inward-oriented."

Over the last two decades Caribbean economists have continued to highlight the importance of exports in Caribbean economies [Farrell (1982), and Worrell (1987)]. Economists point to the high export GDP (Gross Domestic Product) ratios of Caribbean economies. The data in Table 1.1 illustrate the point.

In Table 1.1 export/GDP ratios are high and are at least 60% on average for the four Caribbean countries in the 1968–1990 period. In the two subperiods there is a lot of variation in the ratios for the individual countries. In Barbados and Trinidad and Tobago the export ratios are lower in the 1980–1990 subperiod. The raw annual data reveal that this was largely due to a slowdown in export growth and/or higher GDP in the 1980–1990 subperiod. Although in the case of Barbados, despite the fall in the export ratio, it is still high in 1980–1990 at 65.2%.

In contrast, Guyana and Jamaica experienced increases in their export/GDP ratios in the 1980–1990 subperiod. This was largely due to sharp contractions in nominal GDP rather than increases in total exports. It is also notable that Jamaica no longer had the lowest export/GDP ratio in the 1980–1990 subperiod. Trinidad and Tobago now had the lowest ratio or was the least "open" with an export/GDP ratio of 33.3% in the 1980–1990 subperiod. The significant decline in the export/GDP ratio in Trinidad and Tobago was the result of a substantial contraction in petroleum exports, which accounted for at least 60% of total exports, in the 1980–1990 subperiod.

The Caribbean economies openness to international trade is also manifested in their relatively high import/GDP ratios. The data in Table 1.2 illustrate this

| Table 1.2 Import/GDP Ratios (Averages) in Selected Caribbean Countries (percentages) | | | |
|---|---|---|---|
| Country | 1968–1990 | 1968–1979 | 1980–1990 |
| Barbados | 52.7 | 69.6 | 53.4 |
| Guyana | 57.0 | 58.4 | 67.5 |
| Jamaica | 47.8 | 38.2 | 43.3 |
| Trinidad and Tobago | 41.0 | 50.5 | 36.2 |

**Source:** World Bank (1990a) *World Tables* (1989–1990 edition); and the International Monetary Fund, *International Financial Statistics* (various issues).

point. In the 1968–1990 period the import/GDP ratios range from 41% in Trinidad and Tobago to 57% in Guyana. There is a lot of variation in the import/GDP ratios between the subperiods 1968–1979 and 1980–1990. Similar to the export/GDP ratios one observes that Barbados and Trinidad and Tobago experienced declines in their import/GDP ratios in the 1980–1990 subperiod. Once again the annual data indicates that this is due to a substantial contraction in nominal imports in Trinidad and Tobago at an annual average rate of 7.2%. On the other hand, Barbados's import growth was modest at an annual average rate of 4% but nominal GDP expanded significantly at an annual average rate of 13.6%. Therefore, the base of the ratio (GDP) expanded rapidly, worsening the overall ratio. Notwithstanding these changes the import/GDP ratios in Barbados and Trinidad and Tobago are high.

In the opposite direction, Guyana and Jamaica experienced increases in their import/GDP ratios in the 1980–1990 subperiod, the major factor being the decline in nominal GDP in this subperiod. In Guyana and Jamaica nominal GDP declined at an annual average rate of 3.0% and 2.0%, respectively. The fall in the base (GDP) of the ratio contributed to increasing the overall ratio.

Despite the fluctuations in their import/GDP and export/GDP ratios the CARICOM[1] economies still have relatively high ratios indicative of a high degree of openness to international trade. This is one of the most important economic characteristics of these economies.

In Table 1.3 data are provided on some of the key economic characteristics of the major CARICOM economies. There is not only variation between the countries in their trade ratios but also in their real GDP and per capita real GDP. In 1988 Guyana's per capita real GDP stood at US$136, meaning Guyana can be classified as a low-income developing country. On the other hand, Jamaica, Trinidad and Tobago, and Barbados are regarded as middle-income developing countries. Barbados and Trinidad and Tobago have substantially higher per capita GDP and can be regarded as upper middle-income developing countries.

| Table 1.3 Key Economic Characteristics of Selected Caribbean Countries (1988) | | | | |
|---|---|---|---|---|
| Item | Barbados | Guyana | Jamaica | Trinidad and Tobago |
| Population (millions) | 0.255[1] | 0.799 | 2.429 | 1.241 |
| Real GDP (1980 Prices US$) | 804.95 | 108.7 | 796.3 | 3008.6 |
| Per Capita Real GDP (US$M 1980 prices) | 3154.9 | 136.0 | 327.8 | 2462.0 |
| X/Y (Percent) | 56.4[2] | 64.2 | 53.2 | 33.3 |
| M/Y (Percent) | 36.5 | 57.1 | 45.1 | 26.6 |

**Source:** World Bank (1990a) *World Tables* (1989–1990 edition).

**Notes:** [1]This is an estimate; [2]As stated previously exports of nonfactor services are included given the importance of tourist receipts to total exports in Barbados and Jamaica.

These classifications are based on the definitions in the 1991 World Development Report [World Bank (1991)]. Middle-income economies are those with a GNP (Gross National Product) per capita of more than US$580 but less than US$6,000 in 1989.

Given the importance of exports in CARICOM economies the weak export performance in the last twenty years is a source of great concern to academics and policymakers in particular. The performance of the traditional primary exports and the nontraditional manufactured exports has been weak particularly in the 1980s.[2] All of the major primary exports—bauxite, oil and sugar—have contracted significantly in the 1980s. The evidence of the deterioration in the major CARICOM countries export performance is provided in Chapter 2.

## 1.2  THE KEY ISSUES

The above analysis points to two important, related questions: First, given the importance of exports to the CARICOM economies, what exactly is the role of exports in these economies? Second, what set of factors explain the weak export performance of the last twenty years and what are some of the policy implications? It is the examination of these two critical issues and the absence of any empirical research analyzing the CARICOM countries export performance that provide the principal motivation for this work.

The focus of the empirical research on the above two questions is on Trinidad and Tobago, Barbados, Guyana, and Jamaica in the 1968–1990 period. In many instances data deficiencies make it impossible to include Guyana or use data up to 1990 in the empirical work. The Dominican Republic (a non-CARICOM Caribbean country), Costa Rica and, to a lesser extent, Mauritius are included for comparative purposes in some areas of the empirical research. In addition, in Chapter 4 a sample of small developing countries (including two CARICOM countries) are used in the estimation of a cross-sectional model of exports and growth.

## 1.3 OUTLINE

Chapter 2 provides a detailed description of the export performance of the major CARICOM countries for which detailed data are available—Jamaica, Barbados, and Trinidad and Tobago—in the 1970–1988 period. The choice of period for the analysis is conditioned by the availability of detailed data on the destination of individual merchandise exports. The results of this chapter provide a justification for the later analysis of the export performance.

In Chapter 3 the issue of antiexport bias is analyzed by looking at the behavior of real effective exchange rates in the period 1968–1990. In addition, an institutional analysis of the recent weak export performance is undertaken by focusing on the set of export incentives adopted by CARICOM countries. The policy lessons of the successful east Asian newly industrializing economies (NIEs) point to weaknesses in the set of export policies and institutional support for exports in the CARICOM countries. In this respect some policy changes are suggested in specific areas to facilitate the development of nontraditional exports.

Chapter 4 looks at two alternative propositions about the role of exports in Caribbean-type economies. First, the Feder (1983) "externality" argument is empirically investigated for a sample of small countries (including the CARICOM countries). As the alternative, one can argue that the foreign exchange contribution of exports is the most important role of these small countries. A simple model is built and tested highlighting the importance of foreign exchange flows to output behavior and, in this context, emphasizes the significance of the foreign exchange contribution of exports.

Complementary to the earlier institutional analysis, Chapter 5 presents a model and estimates of export supply for the major CARICOM countries for the period 1968–1990. The model emphasizes the importance of incentives to the performance of nontraditional exports and this is captured by investigating the influence of the real effective exchange rate.

In Chapter 6 the regional dimension of trade and development policy in CARICOM is discussed. The evolution of the regional integration model is analyzed and the contemporary policy regime being pursued is clearly identified. The influence of national structural adjustment programs on the regional integration strategy is also examined. Finally, a possible way forward for the integration movement and the role of export promotion policy at the regional level is also considered.

Finally, in Chapter 7 some suggestions about future areas of research that need to be pursued to further improve our understanding of export performance as well as potentially successful export development policies in Caribbean-type economies are discussed.

## NOTES

1. The CARICOM countries are all of the countries that belong to the Caribbean community—an economic integration movement. The member countries are all of the Commonwealth Caribbean countries.

2. In the case of primary exports the only exception in the period was the "oil boom" in Trinidad and Tobago in the 1975–1982 subperiod related to the OPEC (Organization of Petroleum Exporting Countries) price increases. In addition, tourist receipts in Jamaica and Barbados have increased significantly and helped to offset declining merchandise export earnings.

# 2

## The Caribbean's Export Performance

A disturbing feature of the behavior of Caribbean economies in the last twenty years has been the marked deterioration in the region's export performance. There have been noticeable declines in all of the Caribbean's major primary exports—bauxite, sugar, oil and bananas—and not a lot of success in the development of manufactured exports. The only area of growth has been the tourist industry. Given the trade-oriented nature of the economies and the importance of foreign exchange earnings to production, maintenance of the standard of living and the region's future growth and development are sources of great concern to policymakers.

In this chapter, the Caribbean's recent export performance is described in Section 1. Section 2 is a descriptive analysis of the export performance via the use of nonstochastic techniques that decompose a country's export performance into specific components. The absolute values of changes in export earnings attributed to the different components are expressed as a percentage of the actual increase in the individual country's export earnings in the presentation of the decomposition results. In addition, an attempt is made to investigate empirically the issue of comparative advantage that is a key factor influencing a country's export development. Finally, the two sets of results are assessed in the last section of this chapter.

## 2.1 REVIEW OF THE EXPORT PERFORMANCE

Generally, over the last two decades, the performance of the Caribbean's major merchandise exports—sugar, bananas, bauxite and oil—has been poor, notwithstanding Trinidad and Tobago's windfall gains from the petroleum industry. Manufactured exports increased rapidly in the 1970s (except for Trinidad and Tobago and Guyana) but slowed down in the 1980s with some countries experiencing significant declines. The phenomenal manufactured export growth rate in Barbados, Costa Rica, Jamaica, and the Dominican Republic in 1968–1979 must be placed in the context of the low level of manufacturing activity at the beginning of the period.

The only real positive aspect has been the rapid growth in tourist receipts and the corresponding emergence of the tourist industry as a major supplier of foreign exchange earnings in all cases except Guyana and Trinidad and Tobago.

The data in Table 2.1 provide some basic indicators of balance of payments performance among the major CARICOM countries. The four CARICOM countries except Barbados were characterized by negative GDP and export growth rates in the 1979–1988 subperiod (except for Barbados). In both subperiods, the performance of the Dominican Republic and Costa Rica was superior. The growth rate of import purchasing power was negative in Jamaica, Trinidad and Tobago, and Guyana in the 1968–1979 subperiod but it improved in the case of Jamaica in the 1979–1988 subperiod. The growth rates were positive and increased in the 1979–1988 subperiod in Barbados, Costa Rica and the Dominican Republic. Changes in the terms of trade were negative in all countries in the 1979–1988 subperiod. Long-term capital flows (net) only increased in Barbados and the Dominican Republic between the two subperiods. In short, export growth and other indicators of balance of payments performance tended to worsen for the major CARICOM countries (excluding Barbados) in the 1979–1988 subperiod. The disaggregated data reveal that Barbados's balance of payments performance in most years during 1979–1988 was enhanced by increased external borrowing, foreign exchange earnings from tourism, and prudent fiscal management.

Manufactured exports grew rapidly in the late 1960s and 1970s in all countries except Trinidad and Tobago and Guyana (see Table 2.2). However, in the 1980s the manufacturing sector's export growth rates declined in all of the countries except Trinidad and Tobago. In the case of Costa Rica and the Dominican Republic there was a definite slowdown in manufactured export growth but Costa Rica's manufactured export growth rate was not negative. In Barbados, Guyana and Jamaica there were negative manufactured export growth rates in the 1980s.

On the positive side there was the strong growth in real tourist receipts or the purchasing power of tourist receipts that accompanied the rapid expansion of the tourist industry in the 1980s, except in the case of Trinidad and Tobago (see Table 2.3). In all countries except the Dominican Republic and Barbados, there was a decline in the growth of real tourist receipts in the 1968–1979 period. In this period manufactured exports grew rapidly in all of the countries except Trinidad and Tobago. In the 1979–1988 subperiod

## Table 2.1
## Indicators of Balance of Payments Performance—Selected Caribbean Countries

| Item | Barbados | | Costa Rica[1] | | Dominican Republic | | Guyana | | Jamaica | | Trinidad and Tobago | |
|---|---|---|---|---|---|---|---|---|---|---|---|---|
| | 1968–79 | 1979–88 | 1968–79 | 1979–88 | 1968–79 | 1979–88 | 1968–79 | 1979–88 | 1968–79 | 1979–88 | 1968–79 | 1979–88 |
| Merchandise Export Growth Rate (average annual growth[4] rates; percentages) | -3.6 | 1 | 6.8 | 2.9 | 1.5 | 1 | 0.02 | -1.1 | 0.6 | -1.9 | -4.4 | -4.2 |
| Growth Rate of Import Purchasing Power[2] (percentages) | 1.7 | 7.2 | 2.1 | 2.3 | 0.4 | 3.4 | -4.6 | N.A. | -4.8 | 1 | -5.1 | -4.2 |
| Changes in the Terms of Trade[3] | 28.4 | -9.7 | -18.7 | -12.4 | 17.3 | -15.7 | -41.4 | -3.4 | -2.9 | -13.3 | 5.2 | -22.7 |
| Changes in Long-term Capital Flows (Net) US$ Million | 3.59[5] | 8.89 | 310.9 | 214.8 | 50.8 | 88.2 | -2.8 | N.A. | 135.4 | -39.3 | 351.7 | -363 |
| GDP Growth Rate | 4 | 1.3 | 7.5[6] | 1.3 | 12.5 | N.A. | 2.2 | -1.7 | 1 | -0.07[7] | 5.9 | -2.6[8] |

**Source:** World Bank (1990a) *World Tables* (1989–1990 edition).

**Notes:** [1]Costa Rica is not a Caribbean country but is frequently used in the regional literature for comparative purposes; [2]Import purchasing power is defined as gross foreign exchange flows (i.e., exports of goods and services and long-term capital flows) deflated by the import price index. The *World Tables* (1989–1990) (World Bank 1990a) publishes a similar measure called capacity to import but excludes long-term capital flows; [3]Changes in the terms of trade are calculated as the difference in the index numbers in the specific period; [4]All growth rates in the table are calculated as percentages; [5]1970 is the earliest year for which data is available on long-term capital flows (net) for all countries; [6]Data is only available for real GNP (1980 = 100); [7]1988 is the last year for data on real GDP; [8]1988 is the last year for data on real GDP.

**Table 2.2**
**Growth of Manufactured Exports—Selected Caribbean Countries**
**(Average annual growth in percentage)**

| Country | 1968–1979 | 1979–1988 |
|---|---|---|
| Barbados | 32.7 | -2.5 |
| Costa Rica | 11.5 | 7.3 |
| Dominican Republic | 86.4 | -1.3 |
| Guyana | -1.0 | -9.3 |
| Jamaica | 53.9 | -2.3 |
| Trinidad and Tobago | -0.8 | 11.9 |

**Source:** World Bank (1990a) *World Tables* (1989–1990 edition).

**Table 2.3**
**The Growth of Tourist Receipts[1]—Selected Caribbean Countries**
**(Average annual growth in percentage)**

| Country | 1968–1979 | 1979–1988 |
|---|---|---|
| Barbados | 2.8[2] | 8.1 |
| Costa Rica | -0.5 | 9.2 |
| Dominican Republic | 7.4 | 1.8 |
| Guyana | -5.2 | N.A. |
| Jamaica | -4.4 | 6.3 |
| Trinidad & Tobago | -6.1 | -6.8 |

**Source:** IMF, (various issues) *Yearbook of Balance of Payments Statistics*.

**Notes:** [1]The data are for the purchasing power of tourist receipts, and nominal tourist receipts are deflated by the country's import price index; [2]In the case of Barbados and Costa Rica, 1969 is the earliest year for which data is available.

tourist receipts grew strongly in all of the countries except Trinidad and Tobago and in the same period total merchandise exports and manufactured exports in particular did not perform well.

The strong performance of the tourist industry in the 1980s is also reflected in the changing shares of tourist receipts and merchandise export earnings in total exports of goods and services. The data in Table 2.4 indicate that in the cases of Barbados, Jamaica, and the Dominican Republic there is a continuous

# Table 2.4
## Distribution of Total Exports of Goods and
## Services for Selected Caribbean Countries (percentages)

### BARBADOS

| Year | Merchandise Exports | Tourist Receipts | Other Services | Total Exports |
|------|---------------------|------------------|----------------|---------------|
| 1969 | 40.5 | 40.8 | 18.7 | 100.0 |
| 1980 | 31.5 | 44.1 | 24.4 | 100.0 |
| 1990 | 23.0 | 67.0 | 10.0 | 100.0 |

### COSTA RICA

| Year | Merchandise Exports | Tourist Receipts | Other Services | Total Exports |
|------|---------------------|------------------|----------------|---------------|
| 1969 | 91.2 | 8.4 | 0.4 | 100.0 |
| 1980 | 82.1 | 7.0 | 10.9 | 100.0 |
| 1990 | 71.6 | 19.5 | 7.9 | 100.0 |

### DOMINICAN REPUBLIC

| Year | Merchandise Exports | Tourist Receipts | Other Services | Total Export |
|------|---------------------|------------------|----------------|--------------|
| 1969 | 80.6 | 7.7 | 11.7 | 100.0 |
| 1980 | 73.2 | 13.1 | 13.7 | 100.0 |
| 1990 | 42.4 | 47.6 | 10.0 | 100.0 |

### GUYANA

| Year | Merchandise Exports | Tourist Receipts | Other Services | Total Exports |
|------|---------------------|------------------|----------------|---------------|
| 1969 | 85.1 | 1.4 | 13.5 | 100.0 |
| 1980 | 94.7 | 0.9 | 4.4 | 100.0 |
| 1987 | N.A. | N.A. | N.A. | 100.0 |

### JAMAICA

| Year | Merchandise Exports | Tourist Receipts | Other Services | Total Exports |
|------|---------------------|------------------|----------------|---------------|
| 1969 | 60.6 | 19.5 | 19.9 | 100.0 |
| 1980 | 56.3 | 28.4 | 15.3 | 100.0 |
| 1990 | 43.3 | 51.2 | 5.5 | 100.0 |

### TRINIDAD AND TOBAGO

| Year | Merchandise Exports | Tourist Receipts | Other Services | Total Exports |
|------|---------------------|------------------|----------------|---------------|
| 1969 | 83.4 | 5.3 | 11.3 | 100.0 |
| 1980 | 75.7 | 4.5 | 19.8 | 100.0 |
| 1990 | 83.5 | 5.0 | 11.5 | 100.0 |

**Source:** IMF (various issues) *Yearbook of Balance of Payments Statistics.*

increase in the share of tourist receipts and a decrease in that of merchandise exports. Only in Barbados, Jamaica and the Dominican Republic do tourist receipts achieve the largest proportion of total exports of goods and services.

In Guyana and to a lesser extent Trinidad and Tobago, tourist receipts are only a small fraction of total exports of goods and services. In Costa Rica the share of merchandise exports declined from 91.2% in 1969 to 71.6% in 1990, and tourist receipts increased from 8.4% to 19.5%, respectively. Despite the changing shares, merchandise exports still command a substantial share of total exports of goods and services.

In summary, the merchandise export performance has not been encouraging but tourist receipts have compensated to some extent for declining merchandise exports. The present study recognizes the importance of the tourist industry but is primarily concerned with analyzing the performance of aggregate merchandise exports and nontraditional manufactured exports (e.g., clothing.)

## 2.2  DESCRIPTIVE ANALYSIS OF THE EXPORT PERFORMANCE

A variety of approaches have been adopted in analyzing a country's export performance. Prominent among these have been nonstochastic techniques that attempt to decompose a country's export performance into specific components. Possibly the most widely used technique in this literature has been the constant market share (CMS) model. This technique is employed in this chapter and provides a useful description of the Caribbean's export performance, although it has not been previously employed in the Caribbean region itself.

A key factor underlying the development of exports is the concept of comparative advantage. Standard neoclassical models argue that countries should specialize in international trade in those commodities in which they have a comparative advantage. There have been useful attempts to draw inferences about a country's comparative advantage using ex post facto trade patterns deriving revealed comparative advantage (RCA) indexes. These results can shed some light on vital issues like the exports in which Caribbean countries manifest comparative advantage and how the pattern of comparative advantage has shifted over time in these countries. The RCA analysis is complementary to the decomposition of the export performance. Like the CMS analysis, RCA analysis has not been previously undertaken with Caribbean data. Together, the results of the CMS and RCA analyses should adequately describe the Caribbean's export performance in the last twenty years.

### 2.2a  A Constant Market Share Analysis

Alternatives to time series (regression) analysis of a country's export performance are *decompositions*. Decomposition is a nonstochastic technique that attributes a country's export performance to specific demand and supply factors. The methodology most commonly applied by researchers is a constant market share analysis of export performance. The model was first used by Tyszynski (1951) to analyze changes in the market share of countries exporting manufactures. There have been a variety of applications to developing countries [Banerji (1974), Love (1984)].

In the early works on trade and development there was a literature spawned by the "trade pessimists" that encouraged the adoption of inward-oriented development strategies by many developing countries. The writings of Myrdal (1957), Nurkse (1961), and Prebisch (1964) contended that the prospects for LDCs (Less Developed Countries) export expansion were poor because of unfavorable external demand and domestic supply factors. It was observed that developing country exports did not expand as fast as the world average. This phenomenon was attributable, it was argued, to a combination of three factors. First, developing country exports may be concentrated on commodities for which the world demand is growing more slowly than that of the world average for all commodities. Second, the market distribution of developing country exports may be biased toward markets that are stagnant relative to those in which the demand is growing faster than the world average. Finally, developing countries may be less competitive than developed countries. It was contended that a lack of competitiveness reflects the domestic supply influences and the impact of government policies in developing countries.

The first two factors, explaining the slow growth of developing country exports, are essentially demand-related. Only the last factor focuses on the supply influences inhibiting the growth of developing country exports.

### The CMS Model

The CMS model enables one to split numerically the past growth of a country's exports into the factors outlined above. More specifically, the CMS model can be outlined as follows (see Appendix 2.A.1 for a full derivation of the model):

$$\sum_i (V_i^{(2)} - V_i^{(1)}) = r\, V \ldots + \sum_i (r_i - r)V_i^{(1)} +$$

$$\sum_i \sum_j (r_{ij} - r_i)\, V_{ij}^{(1)} = \sum_i \sum_j (V_{ij}^{(2)} - V_{ij}^{(1)} - r_{ij}V_{ij}^{(1)}). \qquad (1)$$

Where:

$V_i^{(1)}$ = Value of developing country exports of commodity $i$ in Period 1.

$V_i^{(2)}$ = Value of developing country exports of commodity $i$ in Period 2.

$V_{ij}$ = Value of developing country exports of commodity $i$ to market j.

$r$ = Percentage increase in aggregate world trade from period 1 to period 2.

$r_i$ = Percentage increase in the world trade for commodity $i$ from period 1 to period 2.

$r_{ij}$ = Percentage increase in the world export of commodity $i$ to market $j$ from period 1 to period 2.

The superscripts (1) and (2) refer to the initial and the terminal year respectively. An economic interpretation of the various terms in equation (1) is now in order. First, the bracketed term on the left-hand side of the identity indicates the actual change in exports within a specific period. On the right-hand side, the first term indicates what the increase in a country's export earnings would have been had its exports increased at the same rate as the world average; in other words, the increase in a country's export earnings if it had maintained its share of world exports within the period. The second term measures the *commodity composition effect*. This term is a weighted sum of the various exports from a country, but the exports are not differentiated by their regions of destination. The weights that are used are the deviations of the growth rates of individual commodity exports from the growth rate of aggregate world exports. A negative sign for the commodity composition effect would imply that a country had concentrated its exports on commodities whose growth rate was lower than the average growth rate of world exports.

The third term on the right-hand side is defined as the *market distribution effect*. This term allows for the differentiation of exports by commodity and by market. The term is a weighted sum of the values of each export going into each market. The weights are the deviation of the growth rate of a specific market for a particular commodity export from the average growth rate of world exports for that commodity. Two reasons have been advanced for the deviation in growth rates: First, the income elasticity of demand for the same commodity varies across markets; and second, real income growth will vary across countries reflecting different growth rates in demand.

One can interpret a negative market distribution effect as indicating that a country had failed to concentrate on the relatively faster growing areas of world trade. Of course, in the opposite case the market distribution effect would be positive.

The last term in the identity is a residual that shows the difference between the actual growth of developing country exports and what it would have been had the country maintained its world market share, that is, the hypothetical increase in exports. Generally, the term is interpreted as indicating the presence (positive sign) or absence (negative sign) of competitiveness. The interpretation of the residual is a controversial issue in the literature (see Love 1984). In the CMS model that part of the growth of a country's exports that is not explained by the growth of world demand (i.e., components 1 and 2) is assigned to a competitiveness effect. There is no well-articulated theoretical model to explain the residual so the interpretations in the literature are ad hoc. The following interpretation is possible: The share of a country's exports in world exports is a function of supply conditions, including the incentive structure. A negative residual to some extent implies that domestic supply influences and government policies are making a negative impact on export performance.

By definition, this residual effect includes both supply effects and any demand effects not picked up in the necessarily gross measurements affected by the first two categories. In other words, there is no conceptual ambiguity about this residual, just a lack of empirical knowledge as to what its major components are.

The CMS model does not provide a complete analysis of a country's export performance, but it is not different from any other model in this respect. A serious limitation of the model is that it is based upon demand considerations. Future improvements should try to give equal or greater weight to supply influences.

In summary, despite the limitations of the CMS analysis it has been used extensively in studies on developing countries export performance. The results provide a useful description of a country's export performance. In addition the studies also point to some key factors influencing the country's export performance, although strong policy conclusions are not typically drawn from the results.

## 2.2b  Revealed Comparative Advantage Analysis

The commodity pattern of comparative advantage across countries is a central concept in international trade theory. Countries are supposed to specialize in and export those commodities in that they have a comparative advantage. However, the concept of comparative advantage is based upon autarkic prices which are not observable in posttrade equilibrium. Thus, if the concept of comparative advantage is to be used empirically, it must be measured indirectly using posttrade events.

A frequently used measure of comparative advantage ex post facto is the concept of revealed comparative advantage (RCA) introduced by Bela Balassa. RCA relates to the relative trade performances of individual countries in specific commodities. On the assumption that "the commodity pattern of trade reflects intercountry differences in relative costs as well as in non-price factors, this is assumed to 'reveal' the comparative advantage of the trading countries" [Balassa (1965) p. 327].

The purposes of analyzing the context of the Caribbean's export performance are: First, to determine the set of exports in which Caribbean countries have a revealed comparative advantage; Second to examine the commodity composition of Caribbean exports—primary products, labor-intensive manufactures and so on—and how the pattern of comparative advantage shifted over the 1970s and 1980s; Third, to analyze the differences across Caribbean countries both in the commodity composition of exports and the shifts in the pattern of comparative advantage. The results should complement the CMS analysis in painting a true picture of the Caribbean's export performance in the last two decades.

## The RCA Index

The concept of "revealed" comparative advantage is particularly attractive since it is easily quantified in the form of an index that can be used in various types of intercountry and interindustry comparisons.[1]

A country's RCA in the trade of a specific commodity is measured by the share of the commodity in a country's total commodity exports relative to the commodity's share in total world exports. Specifically, if $X_{ij}$ is the value of country $i$'s exports of commodity $j$ and $X_{it}$ is the country's total commodity exports its RCA is:

$$RCA_{ij} = (X_{ij}/(X_{it}/(X_{wj}/X_{wt}), \qquad (1a)$$

where the $w$ subscripts refer to world trade totals.

If the index is less than unity this is interpreted to mean that the country is at a comparative *disadvantage* in the specific commodity under question. However, if the RCA index exceeds unity this indicates that the country has a revealed comparative advantage in that particular commodity. One must be cautious in interpreting RCA indexes as these are based on performance and may not correspond to actual (theoretical) comparative advantage. Generally, RCA analysis cannot tell you about "true" comparative advantage because it is based on performance that may be greatly affected by "distortions" or governmental interventions.

As stated earlier, if an RCA index exceeds unity, the country has a revealed comparative advantage in that commodity. A country's exports can be ranked on the basis of its RCA indexes. The export with the highest RCA index is the export in which the country possesses the strongest revealed comparative advantage. RCA indexes are ordinal measures, thus the rankings of a country's exports based on RCA indexes cannot identify the magnitude of the differences in a country's comparative advantage among industries (Yeats 1985).

RCA indexes are calculated separately for manufactured exports for all three countries (i.e., Jamaica, Barbados and Trinidad and Tobago). Given our intention to look closely at nontraditional exports, it is useful to compute RCA indexes for manufactured exports. The methodology is identical except that only SITC 5—SITC 8 are included and the totals used are for manufactured exports, *not* total exports.

It must be noted that this measure refers to revealed comparative advantage in manufactured exports only. An index number of 110 means that the individual manufactured exports share in the country's total manufactured exports is 10% higher than their share in world manufactured exports.

RCA indexes provide useful insights into a country's exports but they can offer no policy guidance. Therefore, policy conclusions are not usually drawn in these studies.

## 2.3  DATA AND RESULTS

### 2.3a  Data

CMS analysis is undertaken for Jamaica, Barbados and Trinidad and Tobago for the period 1970–1987 and the subperiods 1970–1979 and 1979–1987.[2] The periodization is conditioned by the absence of detailed trade statistics for later years. Furthermore, service exports (mainly tourism) are omitted as they are not available at the level of disaggregation required for CMS analysis. Given their importance and positive contribution to export performance in Jamaica and Barbados, this is a limitation of the analysis.

The year 1979 is treated as a breaking point in the CMS analysis because of the fact that external conditions were different in the two decades (1970s and 1980s): Whereas in the 1970s, where external conditions improved (after the first oil shock), in the 1980s, a period of only moderate world economic growth, slow growth in world trade, and acute economic decline took place in all three Caribbean countries. Furthermore, only Jamaica began to experience economic decline in the later half of the 1970s. On the other hand, Trinidad and Tobago was experiencing a boom owing to strong oil prices, and Barbados's economic performance was satisfactory. In short, the international conditions differed markedly between the two decades and domestic circumstances were also different. In addition, the second oil shock in 1979 was the beginning of the tough economic period for many developing countries.

In the CMS analysis all of the individual countries exports are used in the empirical work over the set of markets for which data are available.[3] The commodities are also arranged in terms of commodity type. (See Appendix 2.A.2 for a list of the commodities and the set of markets used in the analysis for each country.) The classification used was that of Leamer (1984), later modified by Rana (1988).[4] Individual country exports are classified into three types—primary products, crops and animal products, and manufactures. The latter is further classified as labor intensive manufactures, moderately capital/skill intensive manufactures, and highly capital/skill intensive manufactures. In short, exports are classified into five commodity types:

1. Primary products (P)
2. Crops and animal products (CAP)
3. Labor intensive manufactures (LI)
4. Moderately capital/skill intensive manufactures (MCSI)
5. Highly capital/skill intensive manufactures (HCSI)

In the computation of the RCA indexes world data were proxied by the total of the developed market economies obtained from the *U.N. Yearbook of International Trade Statistics*. The data for individual Caribbean commodity exports were obtained from the *U.N. Commodity Trade Statistics* for the years 1970, 1979, and 1987. Three Caribbean countries were in the sample (Jamaica, Barbados, and Trinidad and Tobago). A starting year of 1970 is used as in both the CMS and RCA analyses since this is the first year for which detailed trade data are available.

## 2.3b Results

The CMS and RCA results are presented for each of the individual countries in the sample. Results are presented for both total merchandise exports and manufactured exports.

### Barbados

Table 2.5 shows the results of decomposing the difference between the actual and the hypothetical increase in Barbados's exports into the three effects based on the identity presented earlier. The hypothetical increase in a given period is the amount by which Barbados' export earnings should have increased to have maintained a constant share of the world market.

In the entire 1970–1987 period the hypothetical increase was greater than the actual increase indicating that Barbados lost world market share. The negative divergence between the actual and the hypothetical increase in export earnings is largely due, based on the CMS results, to a loss of competitiveness (i.e., supply considerations), an unfavorable commodity composition of the export basket, and an unfavorable distribution of export markets, in that order of importance. The period is split into two subperiods, 1970–1979 and 1979–1987, to get a greater insight into the country's export performance.

**Table 2.5**
**Constant Market Share Analysis of the Change**
**in Barbados's Exports, 1970–1987, 1970–1979, and 1979–1987**
**(millions of U.S. Dollars; percentage changes in parentheses)**

| Item | 1970–1987 | 1970–1979 | 1979–1987 |
|---|---|---|---|
| (a) Actual Increase in Barbados Exports | 178.607 (100.0) | 89.013 (100.0) | 89.594 (100.0) |
| (b) Hypothetical Increase in Barbados Exports | 391.107 (218.9) | 28.992 (32.6) | 368.155 (410.9) |
| (c) Net Difference | -218.54 | 60.021 | -278.561 |
| (d) Commodity Composition Effect | -98.79 (-55.3) | 43.668 (49.1) | -142.46 (-158.9) |
| (e) Market Distribution Effect | -7.55 (-4.2) | 17.963 (20.2) | -25.503 (-28.5) |
| (f) Competitiveness Effect (Residual) | -112.198 (-63.2) | -1.6 (-1.8) | -110.598 (-123.4) |

**Sources:** Calculated from data taken from the *U.N. Yearbook of International Trade Statistics* and the *U.N. Commodity Trade Statistics.*

In the 1970–1979 period there is a positive divergence between the actual and the hypothetical increase in export earnings. This is largely due, according to estimates based on CMS analysis, to a favorable composition of the export basket and distribution of export markets, but there is some small loss of competitiveness that dampens the export performance.

The results for the period 1979–1987 are in direct contrast to the period 1970–1979. Whereas, the hypothetical increase was less than the actual increase in 1970–1979, the opposite is true in 1979–1987. In 1970–1979 Barbados's exports expanded by more than was necessary to maintain world market share actually increasing its world market share. However, in 1979–1987 these early gains were lost and Barbados's exports increased by less than what was necessary to maintain world market share. The shifts in the components in the later period are also interesting. First, there is a complete reversal in the commodity composition effect. It is still relatively the most important component (-158.8%), but it is now negative. Second, the market distribution effect is now negative and the least important of the components of export performance. Finally, the large negative residual indicates an increased loss of competitiveness of exports. The competitiveness effect also increased in relative importance as a component of the export performance. Note that over the entire 1970–1987 period the competitiveness effect, that is, supply influences, was the most important component of the export performance.

Table 2.1 shows that Barbados's merchandise export performance improved in the 1979–1988 subperiod, but the CMS analysis indicates that all of the components of the export performance were negative in the subperiod. This apparent contradiction is due to the fact that merchandise exports—mainly sugar, clothing, and electronics—improved their performance in the 1978–1985 period but deteriorated sharply thereafter. The CMS analysis picks this up but the growth rates for merchandise exports do not.

The above analysis only considers merchandise exports and *not* services. However, in the period 1979–1987 tourist receipts became the major export earner for Barbados. Therefore, an analysis of Barbados's export performance must consider the performance of the tourist industry. In the 1970–1979 period the purchasing power of tourist receipts (nominal tourist receipts deflated by the import price index) increased at an annual average rate of 45.6% and in 1979–1987 at a rate of 6.3%. The performance of tourism earnings compensated for the weaknesses in merchandise export performance in the latter period, and tourist receipts accounted for at least 60% of total export earnings, therefore cushioning the economy against significant shortfalls in total exports of goods. Notwithstanding this, one still has to be concerned about the significant deterioration in the merchandise export performance.

The CMS exercise is repeated for manufactured exports, and the results, presented in Table 2.6, show that for the whole period 1970–1987 the hypothetical increase in manufactured exports was greater than the actual increase in manufactured exports indicating a loss of world market share. The negative divergence between the hypothetical and the actual increase is attributable to a loss of competitiveness or supply considerations, an unfavorable commodity composition of exports, and an unfavorable distribution of export markets, in that order of importance.

In the 1970–1979 subperiod the hypothetical increase was less than the actual increase in manufactured exports, but this was completely reversed in 1979–1987. Consistent with the results for total exports, this implies that manufactured exports expanded by more than was necessary to maintain world market share in 1970–1979, with the situation reversing itself in 1979–1987.

The positive divergence between the actual increase and the hypothetical increase in 1970–1979 was due to a favorable composition of Barbados's export manufacturing basket, competitiveness in manufacturing exports, and a favorable distribution of manufacturing exports based on markets, in that order of importance. In contrast, the CMS analysis for the 1979–1987 period reveals striking differences. First, the difference between the actual increase and the constant share norm (hypothetical) increase reversed itself and Barbados's manufactured exports expanded by less than was necessary to maintain world market share. Second, the turnaround in manufactured export performance was largely due to a loss of competitiveness in manufactured exports. In the 1970–1987 period the competitiveness effect or supply consideration was the

**Table 2.6**
**Constant Market Share Analysis of the Change in Barbados's**
**Manufactured Exports, 1970–1987, 1970–1979, and 1979–1987**
**(millions of U.S. dollars; percentage changes in parentheses)[1]**

| Item | 1970–1987 | 1970–1979 | 1979–1987 |
|---|---|---|---|
| (a) Actual Increase in Barbados Manufacturing Exports | 174.739 (100.0) | 53.671 (100.0) | 121.068 (100.0) |
| (b) Hypothetical Increase in Barbados Manufacturing Exports | 307.064 (175.7) | 9.587 (18.9) | 297.477 (245.7) |
| (c) Net Difference | -132.325 | 44.084 | -176.409 |
| (d) Commodity Composition Effect | -11.305 (-6.5) | 26.221 (48.8) | -37.526 (-31.0) |
| (e) Market Distribution Effect | -2.465 (-1.41) | 3.321 (6.2) | -5.786 (-4.8) |
| (f) Competitiveness Effect (Residual) | -118.553 (-67.8) | 14.542 (27.1) | -133.1 (-109.9) |

**Sources:** Calculated from data taken from the *U.N. Yearbook of International Trade Statistics* and the *U.N. Commodity Trade Statistics*.

**Note:** [1]Manufactured exports are computed as the total of SITC 5 to SITC 8.

most important component of the manufactured export performance. The evidence implies that Barbados needs to look at its incentives to manufactured exports. Third, the commodity composition effect was now negative, indicating an unfavorable composition of the manufactured export basket and the need for a restructuring of the manufactured export sector. Finally, the market distribution effect also became negative, but was only a small percentage (-4.8%) of the actual increase in manufactured exports and, therefore, it does not merit further consideration.

In short, the CMS analysis of the manufactured export performance is broadly consistent with that of total exports, but there are differences in the behavior of the various components across the time periods. In addition, the results reflect an annual average decline in manufactured exports of 3.9% in the period 1979–1987. Notably, there was a decline in clothing exports (a key nontraditional export) at an annual average rate of 2.4%. The evidence points to the need for urgent policy attention aimed at identifying and initiating "new" manufactured exports with positive long-term prospects.

In Table 2.7 the top ten exports (based on RCA indexes) are presented for Barbados for the years 1970, 1979, and 1987. In the period 1970–1979, Barbados appeared to have some noticeable shifts in its pattern of comparative advantage. In 1970 Barbados had revealed comparative advantage in crops and

| Table 2.7 |
| :---: |
| **Top Ten Items in RCA Vector for Barbados—** |
| **1970, 1979, and 1987[1]** |

| BARBADOS | |
| :---: | :---: |
| **Commodity Type** | **1970** |
| CAP | Sugar and Honey |
| CAP | Margarine, Shortening |
| CAP | Fish and Preparations |
| CAP | Alcoholic Beverages |
| CAP | Cereal Preparations etc. |
| MCSI | Electrical Machinery* |
| HCSI | Pigments, Paints etc.* |
| HCSI | Perfume, Cosmetics etc.* |
| LI | Textile Products etc.* |
| LI | Clothing not of fur* |
| **Commodity Type** | **1979** |
| CAP | Sugar and Honey |
| CAP | Margarine, Shortening |
| LI | Articles of Plastic etc.* |
| LI | Clothing not of fur* |
| LI | Toys, Sporting Goods etc.* |
| MCSI | Electrical Machinery* |
| HCSI | Plastic Materials etc.* |
| CAP | Cereal Preparations etc. |
| CAP | Alcoholic Beverages |
| HCSI | Soaps, Cleaning etc. Preparations* |
| **Commodity Type** | **1987** |
| LI | Transistors, Valves etc.* |
| CAP | Margarine, Shortening |
| CAP | Sugar and Honey |
| LI | Cement, Building Products etc.* |
| HCSI | Pesticides, Disinfectants* |
| LI | Women's Outerwear not knit* |
| P | Stone, Sand and Gravel |
| CAP | Alcoholic Beverages |
| HCSI | Perfume, Cosmetics etc.* |
| HCSI | Soaps, Cleaning etc. Preparations* |

**Sources:** Calculated from data taken from the *U.N. Yearbook of International Trade Statistics* and the *U.N. Commodity Trade Statistics*.

**Notes:** [1]Items are listed in descending order, i.e., from highest to lowest indexes in the top ten; Asterisks refer to manufactured exports.

animal products (CAP) and some moderately(MCSI)/highly(HCSI) capital or skill intensive products. In 1979 one observed "revealed" comparative advantage over a wider range of product types particularly in labor intensive manufactures (LI). In 1979 Barbados lost revealed comparative advantage in fish and

*Barbados*

preparations; pigments, paints etc.; perfumes, cosmetics etc.; and textile products, while gaining in articles of plastic; toys, sporting goods etc.; plastic materials; and soaps. The shifts in the pattern of comparative advantage appear to reflect a restructuring of exports in response to changes in underlying factors—wage costs (factor prices), technical change, and so forth.

In 1987 there was some loss of revealed comparative advantage in labor intensive manufactures, particularly in articles of plastic and toys, sporting goods, and so on. But RCA was gained in transistors, valves etc.; cement, building products etc.; pesticides, disinfectants; and stone, sand, and gravel. Moderately/highly capital or skill intensive manufactures still feature prominently in the top ten export items. Therefore, revealed comparative advantage is still evident in manufactured exports, but probably more so in moderately/highly capital or skill intensive manufactured exports. One should note that in 1987 the top export item based on RCA indexes was in the electronics sector—transistors, valves, etc. However, since 1987 the INTEL Corporation, which was largely responsible for Barbados's electronics exports, closed its operations in Barbados and electronics exports contracted significantly. A variety of explanations have been advanced to explain the closure of INTEL. The most widely accepted factors are: First, labor costs in Barbados had become uncompetitive relative to other developing countries, inducing foreign investors to seek lower cost locations. Second, technological change in the electronics industry had resulted in process innovations that removed the cost advantage of labor intensive processes in some areas. The impact of INTEL's closure on Barbados's manufactured exports was devastating. Barbados's manufactured exports declined from US$188 million in 1986 to US$96 million in 1987.

By 1987 Barbados had lost its revealed comparative advantage in some exports of crops and animal products and labor intensive manufactures. Moderately capital/skill intensive manufactured exports (MCSI) and, to a lesser extent, HCSI exports, were the areas in which Barbados had apparently gained revealed comparative advantage. The deteriorating export performance of the 1979–1987 period reflects the need to stimulate the development of these export activities, particularly the supply-side rattio constraints to their expansion.

Given the importance of manufactured exports, RCA indexes were calculated separately for Barbados's manufactured exports. In Table 2.8 the top ten manufactured exports (based on RCA indexes) are presented for the years 1970, 1979, and 1987. Barbados's revealed comparative advantage is spread across all three manufactured product types but labor intensive manufactures are most important. Electronic and clothing exports appear to be the areas in which Barbados has a continuing revealed comparative advantage. However, as stated earlier, the electronics industry was dominated prior to 1987 by a large foreign firm (the INTEL Corporation). Officials at the Industrial Development Corporation also point to a significant number of other plant closures in the textile

*Also*

**Table 2.8**
**Top Ten Items in RCA Vector (Manufactured Exports)**
**for Barbados—1970, 1979, and 1987[1]**

| BARBADOS | |
|---|---|
| **Commodity Type** | **1970** |
| MCSI | Electrical Machinery |
| HCSI | Pigments, Paints etc. |
| LI | Textile Products |
| HCSI | Perfume, Cosmetics etc. |
| LI | Clothing not of fur |
| HCSI | Soaps, Cleaning etc. Preparation |
| LI | Articles of Paper |
| LI | Gold, Silverware, Jewelry |
| LI | Cement, Building Products etc. |
| MCSI | Structures and Parts etc. |
| **Commodity Type** | **1979** |
| LI | Clothing not of fur |
| MCSI | Electrical Machinery |
| LI | Toys, Sporting Goods etc. |
| HCSI | Perfume, Cosmetics etc. |
| LI | Clay, Refectory Building Products |
| LI | Textile Products |
| MCSI | Structures and Parts etc. |
| HCSI | Soaps, Cleaning etc. Preparations |
| HCSI | Pigments, Paints etc. |
| LI | Articles of Plastic etc. |
| **Commodity Type** | **1987** |
| LI | Transistors, Values etc. |
| LI | Textile Clothing Accessories, etc. |
| LI | Cement, Building Products etc. |
| MCSI | Switchgear etc. Parts |
| LI | Under Garments Knitted |
| HCSI | Pesticides, Disinfectants |
| HCSI | Soaps, Cleaning etc. Preparations |
| LI | Women's Outerwear, not knit |
| LI | Articles of Paper etc. |
| HCSI | Perfume, Cosmetics etc. |

**Sources:** Calculated from data taken from the *U.N. Yearbook of International Trade Statistics* and the *U.N. Commodity Trade Statistics*.

**Note:** [1]These top ten items were derived using RCA indexes computed from total manufactured exports.

and clothing industry since 1987, particularly the major foreign firms exporting largely to the U.S. market.[5]

The CMS analysis indicates that supply considerations were the key factor in explaining Barbados's manufactured export performance in the 1970–1987 period and the 1979–1987 subperiod. The recent plant closures in the clothing and electronics industries suggest that Barbados may need to improve its incentives to the manufacturing sector, particularly moderately capital/skill

*supply considerations key factor*

**Table 2.9**
**Constant Market Share Analysis of Sources of Change in Trinidad and Tobago's Total Exports, 1970–1987, 1970–1979, and 1979–1987 (millions of U.S. dollars; percentage changes in parentheses)**

| Item | 1970–1987 | 1970–1979 | 1979–1987 |
|---|---|---|---|
| (a) Actual Increase in Trinidad and Tobago's Exports | 3277.9 (100.0) | 2129.90 (100.0) | 1148.0 (100.0) |
| (b) Hypothetical Increase in Trinidad and Tobago's Total Exports | 8497.8 (259.2) | 457.0 (21.5) | 8040.8 (700.4) |
| (c) Net Difference | -5220.8 | 1672 | -6892.8 |
| (d) Commodity Composition Effect | -5328.19 (-159.3) | 2050.01 (96.3) | -7378.2 (-642.7) |
| (e) Market Distribution Effect | 874.798 (26.7) | 1650.0 (77.5) | -775.202 (-67.5) |
| (f) Competitiveness Effect | -767.41 (-23.4) | -2028.01 (-95.2) | -1260.6 (109.8) |

**Sources:** Calculated from data taken from the *U.N. Yearbook of International Trade Statistics* and the *U.N. Commodity Trade Statistics.*

intensive-type activities. Other "nonprice" supply influences that affect manu-factured export performance may also need to be addressed (e.g., export marketing arrangements, trade financing and the efficiency of customs proce-dures).

### Trinidad and Tobago

The results of the CMS analysis of export performance in Trinidad and Tobago over the period 1970–1987, and subperiods 1970–1979 and 1979–1987, are presented in Table 2.9. In the 1970–1987 period the large diver-gence between the actual increase and hypothetical increase in exports is attributable to an unfavorable commodity composition of exports, a favor-able distribution of export markets, and a loss of competitiveness, in that order of importance.

In the 1970–1979 subperiod there is a positive divergence between the actual increase and the hypothetical increase in exports. This was largely the result of, first, a favorable composition of the export basket, and second, a negative competitive effect that had an unfavorable impact on Trinidad and Tobago's export performance. The importance of supply consideration in the export performance of the 1970–1979 period is consistent with the results for the 1970–1987 period. In addition, there was a favorable distribution of export markets.

In Table 2.1 Trinidad and Tobago's merchandise export growth rate was −4.4% in the subperiod 1968–1979. The strong export performance in the CMS analysis for 1970–1979, using current price data, reflected favorable changes in the terms of trade stimulated by sharp increases in oil prices in 1974.

A closer look at Trinidad and Tobago's export performance provides some insight into the results of the CMS analysis. Trinidad and Tobago's export earnings are heavily dependent on fuel export receipts. Fuel exports accounted for 77.2% of total exports in 1970, 90.8% in 1979, and 71.1% in 1987. Given such a heavy dependence on fuel exports, Trinidad and Tobago's export performance is highly correlated with the performance of fuels. In the period 1970–1979 fuel exports grew at an average annual rate of 53.7% and in 1979–1987 declined at an average annual rate of 6.2%. The strong export performance in the 1970–1979 period, observed from the CMS analysis, is reflecting the export performance of the oil industry stimulated by favorable terms of trade changes (see Table 2.1). One must therefore be cautious in drawing conclusions from these aggregate data about the performance of nonoil exports.

The results from the CMS analysis changed markedly in the 1979–1987 period. Generally, the hypothetical increase in exports was greater than the actual increase: Trinidad and Tobago's exports grew more slowly than the rate required to maintain a constant market share. This reversal in the country's export performance is attributable to an unfavorable composition of the export basket, a distinct improvement in competitiveness, and an unfavorable distribution of export markets, in that order of importance. The competitiveness effect, now having a positive sign, was less unfavorable than in the 1970–1979 period, and there was a significant change in its relative importance in both subperiods. In the 1979–1987 period policy responses to balance of payments disequilibrium impacted upon the incentive structure facing exports (e.g., devaluation), the phased removal of direct controls on imports, new fiscal incentives toward exports, and reduced exchange control procedures for exporters. These policy changes had some impact on the competitiveness of Trinidad and Tobago's exports. Given the dominance of oil in Trinidad and Tobago's total exports, the CMS analysis is repeated for nonoil exports and the results are presented in Table 2.10.

In the 1970–1987 period the large divergence between the actual increase and hypothetical increase in nonoil exports is attributable to an unfavorable commodity composition of exports, a loss of competitiveness, and a favorable distribution of export markets, in that order of importance.

In the 1970–1979 subperiod there is a positive divergence between the actual increase and hypothetical increase in nonoil exports, and this is consistent with the CMS results for total exports. The divergence was the result of, first, a favorable composition of the export basket, and second, a negative competitive

**Table 2.10**
**Constant Market Share Analysis of Sources**
**of Change in Trinidad and Tobago's Nonoil Merchandise Exports,**
**1970–1987, 1970–1979, and 1979–1987 (millions of U.S. dollars;**
**percentage changes in parentheses)**

| Item | 1970–1987 | 1970–1979 | 1979–1987 |
|------|-----------|-----------|-----------|
| (a) Actual Increase in Trinidad and Tobago's nonoil exports | 327.5 | 150.9 | 176.62 |
| (b) Hypothetical increase in Trinidad and Tobago's nonoil exports | 865.4 | 95.2 | 770.2 |
| (c) Net Difference | -537.9 | 55.7 | -593.6 |
| (d) Commodity Composition Effect | -328.5 (-100.3) | 223.9 (148.7) | -552.4 (-312.8) |
| (e) Market Distribution Effect | 51.2 (15.6) | 42.6 (21.3) | 8.6 (4.8) |
| (f) Competitiveness Effect | -260.6 (-80.3) | -210.8 (-142.3) | -49.8 (-28.2) |

**Sources:** Calculated from data taken from the *U.N. Yearbook of International Trade Statistics* and the *U.N. Commodity Trade Statistics.*

effect that had an adverse impact on nonoil export performance. In addition, there was a favorable distribution of export markets.

Consistent with the CMS results for total exports, there was a marked change in nonoil export performance in the 1979–1987 subperiod. Generally, the hypothetical increase in nonoil exports was greater than the actual increase, which meant Trinidad and Tobago lost world market share. This significant change in Trinidad and Tobago's nonoil export performance was attributable to an unfavorable composition of the export market, an improvement in competitiveness, given that the size of the negative sign decreased, and a favorable distribution of export markets. The improvement in competitiveness is to some extent correlated to the adjustment measures mentioned earlier, which were introduced to correct internal and external disequilibrium. In addition, the gains in competitiveness in nonoil exports is consistent with the results for total exports.

The CMS analysis was also repeated for manufactured exports for the period 1970–1987, and the two subperiods 1970–1979 and 1979–1987. The results are presented in Table 2.11. Generally, the manufactured export performance for the entire 1970–1987 period was weak. The large divergence between the actual increase and hypothetical increase in manufactured exports is attributable to an unfavorable commodity composition of exports, loss of competitiveness, and

| Table 2.11<br>Constant Market Share Analysis of<br>Sources of Change in Trinidad and Tobago's<br>Manufactured Exports, 1970–1987, 1970–1979, and 1979–1987<br>(millions of U.S. dollars; percentage changes in parentheses)[1] | | | |
|---|---|---|---|
| Item | 1970–1987 | 1970–1979 | 1979–1987 |
| (a) Actual Increase in Trinidad and Tobago's Manufactured Exports | 291.18<br>(100.0) | 103.18<br>(100.0) | 188.0<br>(100.0) |
| (b) Hypothetical Increase in Trinidad and Tobago's Manufactured Exports | 772.32<br>(265.2) | 53.720<br>(52.1) | 718.6<br>(382.2) |
| (c) Net Difference | -481.14 | 49.46 | -530.6 |
| (d) Commodity Composition Effect | -321.18<br>(-110.3) | 54.22<br>(52.5) | -375.4<br>(-199.6) |
| (e) Market Distribution Effect | -21.05<br>(-7.2) | -10.62<br>(-10.2) | 10.43<br>(-3.9) |
| (f) Competitiveness Effect | -138.91<br>(-47.7) | 5.86<br>(5.7) | -144.77<br>(-77.0) |

**Sources:** Calculated from data taken from the *U.N. Yearbook of International Trade Statistics* and the *U.N. Commodity Trade Statistics*.

**Note:** [1]Manufactured exports are computed as the total of SITC 5 to SITC 8.

an unfavorable distribution of export markets, in that order of importance. In contrast to the total export performance, supply considerations are more important to the manufactured export performance in the 1970–1987 period.

Consistent with the overall export performance, one finds that the manufactured export performance reversed itself over the two subperiods—1970–1979 and 1979–1987.[6] In the latter subperiod, the hypothetical increase in exports was greater than the actual increase in 1979–1987. The favorable commodity composition effect in 1970–1979 became negative in 1979–1987, but remained the most important component of the export performance. The competitiveness effect became negative in 1979–1987 and increased in importance as a factor affecting the export performance. Finally, the market distribution of exports was unfavorable over both periods.

In summary, Trinidad and Tobago's export performance deteriorated from 1970–1979 to 1979–1987 for total merchandise exports and manufactured exports. In both subperiods the commodity composition effect was of prime importance. Its change from a favorable to an unfavorable effect is correlated to the declining fortunes of the oil industry. As stated earlier, fuel exports are at least 70% of Trinidad and Tobago's total exports in the 1970–1987 period. The distinct improvement in the competitiveness effect or supply-side factors (except for manufactured exports) is encouraging and correlated to some extent to the new policy measures. The market distribution effect was the least important component of the export performance.

In Table 2.12 the top ten exports based on RCA indexes are presented for Trinidad and Tobago for the years 1970, 1979, and 1987. The RCA indexes indicate that Trinidad and Tobago lost revealed comparative advantage in some of its exports in the period 1970–1979—inorganic chemicals; inorganic elements, oxides etc.; food preparations; cocoa; fertilizers, manufactured; cement, building products; and metal tanks, boxes etc. Revealed comparative advantage was acquired in other organic chemicals and residual petroleum products. Therefore, Trinidad and Tobago had relatively more unfavorable than favorable shifts in the number of commodities with revealed comparative advantage in the period 1970–1979.

The obvious question is, why does one observe these unfavorable shifts in RCA in Trinidad and Tobago in the 1970–1979 period? One observes that the export sector is dominated by one primary export—crude oil. As stated earlier fuel exports accounted for 77.2% and 90.8% of total merchandise exports in Trinidad and Tobago in 1970 and 1979 respectively. In 1970–1979 oil exports grew at an annual average rate of 53.7%. Given the dependence on crude oil exports and the boom in the petroleum sector in the period, one suspects that there were adverse effects on the rest of the domestic economy, including nonoil exports. Hilaire (1989) argued that the oil boom in the 1970s induced substantial wage increases in the oil sector that stimulated economywide wage increases, resulting in increased domestic costs that is, "Dutch disease" effects. The rise in domestic costs negatively affected Trinidad and Tobago's competitiveness in the export sector in the 1970s. This is a possible explanation for the unfavorable shifts in RCA rankings and the small number of commodities with an RCA greater than unity in 1979.

The earlier CMS results indicate that there was a negative competitiveness effect in the 1970–1979 period that was an important component of Trinidad and Tobago's export performance. The results of the RCA analysis for 1970 and 1979 are consistent with the CMS results for the period. Both sets of results point to the importance of supply considerations in Trinidad and Tobago's export performance.

In 1987 Trinidad and Tobago exhibited revealed comparative advantage in a wider range of exports than it did in 1979. Notably, labor intensive manufactured exports do not appear in the top ten exports based on the RCA indexes. Primary products and crops and animal products still feature prominently in the top ten items. In contrast to 1979, there is an increased number of moderately/highly capital or skill intensive manufactured exports in 1987. One suspects that after the oil boom of the 1970s the economy recovered from the adverse Dutch disease-type effects on the nonoil export sector. Furthermore, it is important to recognize that in response to declining oil output and exports,

| Table 2.12 Top Ten Items in RCA Vector for Trinidad and Tobago—1970, 1979, and 1987 | |
|---|---|
| **TRINIDAD AND TOBAGO** | |
| **Commodity Type** | **1970** |
| HCSI | Coal, Petroleum etc. Chemicals* |
| P | Petroleum (crude) |
| HCSI | Inorganic Elements, Oxides, etc.* |
| CAP | Food Preparations etc. |
| CAP | Cocoa |
| HCSI | Fertilizers, manufactured* |
| LI | Cement, Building Products etc.* |
| MCSI | Structures and Parts etc.* |
| P | Petroleum Products |
| CAP | Sugar and Honey |
| **Commodity Type** | **1979¹** |
| P | Petroleum (crude) |
| P | Residual Petroleum Products |
| HCSI | Other Organic Chemical* |
| P | Petroleum Products |
| HCSI | Inorganic Chemicals* |
| CAP | Sugar and Honey |
| **Commodity Type** | **1987** |
| HCSI | Inorganic Chemicals* |
| P | Petroleum (crude) |
| HCSI | Hydrocarbons, etc. derivatives* |
| MCSI | Iron, Steel Shapes etc.* |
| HCSI | Fertilizers, manufactured* |
| P | Petroleum Products |
| CAP | Sugar and Honey |
| CAP | Other Cereal Meals, Flour |
| CAP | Cereal Preparations etc. |
| CAP | Margarine, Shortening |

**Sources:** Calculated from data taken from the *U.N. Yearbook of International Trade Statistics* and the *U.N. Commodity Trade Statistics*.

**Notes:** There are only six items with an RCA greater then unity; Asterisks refer to manufactured exports.

Trinidad and Tobago introduced a range of adjustment policies. Initially, in 1985 the government devalued the exchange rate, froze public sector wages and removed subsidies on key food items. Subsequently, in 1987 the government began to implement a structural adjustment program in agreement with the IMF

(International Monetary Fund) that included another devaluation, relaxation of import controls, public sector wage cuts, tax reform, and significant cuts in public expenditure. One of the key objectives of these policy changes since 1985 was the stimulation of nonoil exports. These policy shifts contributed in some measure to the changes that occurred in the export sector between 1979–1987, as manifested by the changes in the composition of the top ten export items based on RCA indexes. The CMS results for the 1979–1987 period point to a complete reversal of the negative competitiveness effect indicating improved supply conditions. The results for the RCA indexes in 1987 are consistent with the CMS results for total merchandise exports and manufactured exports.

The top ten items based on RCA indexes for manufactured exports are presented in Table 2.13. The list obviously includes the manufactured exports from Table 2.12 plus additional manufactured exports based on the new RCA indexes. The results in Table 2.13 indicate that the highly capital or skill intensive manufactured exports appear to be the products in which Trinidad and Tobago's revealed comparative advantage, based on manufactured exports, is strongest. However, there is revealed comparative advantage in the labor intensive area as well. In 1970 and 1979 the chemical industry—petrochemicals and soaps and cleaning preparations—and the fertilizer industry were the areas with the highest RCA rankings based on manufactured exports. However, in 1987 the iron and steel industry also became prominent in the RCA rankings based on manufactured exports. As suggested earlier, some proportion of the "windfall" gain in foreign exchange earnings from the oil boom of the 1970s was used to create capital intensive manufactured exports, including iron and steel.[7]

The labor intensive areas that are highest in the RCA rankings, based on manufactured exports for Trinidad and Tobago, are not from the clothing or electronics industries, as was the case in Barbados. The important areas are glassware, building products, and articles of paper.

### Jamaica

The CMS analysis is repeated for Jamaica for the period 1970–1987 and the two subperiods 1970–1979 and 1979–1987. The results are presented in Table 2.14. Jamaica's export performance is not particularly good over either the entire period 1970–1987 or the two subperiods. In the 1970–1987 period there is a large divergence (which is negative) between the actual increase and the hypothetical increase in total exports. This is the result of a loss of competitiveness or supply factors, a favorable commodity composition effect, and an unfavorable distribution of export markets, in that order of importance.

The negative divergence between the actual and the hypothetical increase in the 1970–1979 period is due to a loss of competitiveness, a favorable commodity composition of exports and an unfavorable distribution of export

| Table 2.13 Top Ten Items in RCA Vector (Manufactured Exports) for Trinidad and Tobago—1970, 1979, and 1987 | |
| --- | --- |
| TRINIDAD AND TOBAGO | |
| **Commodity Type** | **1970** |
| HCSI | Coal, Petroleum etc. Chemicals |
| HCSI | Inorganic Elements, Oxides, etc. |
| HCSI | Soaps, Cleaning etc. Preparations |
| HCSI | Fertilizers, manufactured |
| LI | Cement, Building Products etc. |
| MCSI | Metal Tanks, Boxes etc. |
| HCSI | Perfume, Cosmetics etc. |
| LI | Articles of Paper |
| HCSI | Pigments, Paints etc. |
| LI | Gold, Silverware, Jewelry |
| **Commodity Title** | **1979** |
| HCSI | Inorganic Chemicals |
| MCSI | Metal Tanks, Boxes etc. |
| HCSI | Other organic Chemicals |
| HCSI | Soaps, Cleaning etc. Preparations |
| HCSI | Fertilizers, manufactured |
| LI | Other Manufactured Goods |
| LI | Articles of Paper |
| LI | Glassware |
| LI | Under Garments not knit |
| HCSI | Perfume, Cosmetics etc. |
| **Commodity Type** | **1987** |
| HCSI | Inorganic Chemicals |
| HCSI | Hydrocarbons, etc. derivatives |
| MCSI | Iron, Steel Shapes etc. |
| HCSI | Fertilizers, manufactured |
| LI | Cement, Building Products etc. |
| LI | Glassware |
| LI | Other Manufactured Goods |
| LI | Articles of Paper |
| MCSI | Iron, Steel Primary Forms |
| LI | Printed Matter |

**Sources:** Calculated from data taken from the *U.N. Yearbook of International Trade Statistics* and the *U.N. Commodity Trade Statistics*.

markets. In the 1979–1987 subperiod the competitiveness effect has a larger negative sign and remains the most important component cause of the export performance. The commodity composition effect is now negative but remains the second most important component. Finally, the market distribution

**Table 2.14**
**Constant Market Share Analysis of Sources of Change in Jamaica's Total Exports, 1970–1987, 1970–1979, and 1979–1987 (millions of U.S. dollars; percentage changes in parentheses)**

| Item | 1970–1987 | 1970–1979 | 1979–1987 |
|---|---|---|---|
| (a) Actual Increase in Jamaica's Total Exports | 121.795 (100.0) | 395.6 (100.0) | -273.805 (-100.0) |
| (b) Hypothetical Increase in Jamaica's Total Exports | 3222.321 (2645.7) | 730.884 (184.7) | 2491.437 (909.9) |
| (c) Net Difference | -3100.526 | -335.28 | -2765.242 |
| (d) Commodity Composition Effect | 429.164 (352.3) | 910.559 (230.2) | -481.395 (-175.8) |
| (e) Market Distribution Effect | -387.285 (-317.9) | -237.9 (-60.1) | -149.385 (-54.5) |
| (f) Competitiveness Effect | -3142.363 (-2580.0) | -1007.9 (-254.8) | -2134.4627 (-779.5) |

**Source:** Calculated from data taken from the *U.N. Yearbook of International Trade Statistics* and the *U.N. Commodity Trade Statistics*.

effect was negative over both periods, but there was a marginal decrease in its size in the 1979–1987 period.

The poor performance of Jamaica's exports is largely the result of the weak performance of its two major primary exports—bauxite and sugar—and, to a lesser extent, its manufactured exports. Bauxite and sugar comprised 70.3% and 21.7% respectively of total exports in 1970, 71.8% and 7.3% in 1979, and 54.1% and 9.3% in 1987. Bauxite exports grew at an average annual rate of 1.6% between 1970–1979, but declined at a rate of 5.6% in the 1979–1987 period. Sugar exports declined at an average annual rate of 6.1% and 1.8% over the periods 1970–1979 and 1979–1987, respectively.

Jamaica's export performance is not completely captured by the CMS analysis, since tourist receipts achieved an increasingly important share of total exports of goods and services over the period 1970–1987, particularly in the 1980s. In 1979 tourist receipts were 28.4% of total exports of goods and services and reached 49.7% by 1987. In the same period (1979–1987) tourist receipts grew at an annual average rate of 15%. Therefore, the performance of the tourism sector does not mirror the total export performance, and its inclusion improves the overall performance to some degree.

The CMS analysis is repeated for Jamaica's manufactured exports and the results are presented in Table 2.15. The divergence (which is negative) between the actual and the hypothetical increase in the 1970–1987 period is attributable

**Table 2.15**
**Constant Market Share Analysis of Sources of Change in Jamaica's Manufactured Exports, 1970–1987, 1970–1979, and 1979–1987 (millions of U.S. dollars; percentage changes in parentheses)[1]**

| Item | 1970–1987 | 1970–1979 | 1979–1987 |
|---|---|---|---|
| (a) Actual Increase in Jamaica's Manufacturing Exports | 75.94 (100.0) | 44.89 (100.0) | 31.05 (100.0) |
| (b) Hypothetical Increase in Jamaica's Manufacturing Exports | 296.79 (390.8) | 14.28 (48.2) | 282.51 (909.8) |
| (c) Net Difference | -220.85 | 30.56 | -251.46 |
| (d) Commodity Composition Effect | -60.64 (-80.0) | 31.45 (70.1) | -92.09 (-296.6) |
| (e) Market Distribution Effect | -224.06 (-295.05) | -72.6 (-161.7) | -151.46 (-487.8) |
| (f) Competitiveness Effect | 63.8 (84.0) | 71.71 (123.5) | -7.91 (-25.5) |

**Sources:** Calculated from data taken from the *U.N. Yearbook of International Trade Statistics* and the *U.N. Commodity Trade Statistics.*

**Notes:** [1]Manufactured exports are computed as the total of SITC 5 to SITC 8. One should note that aluminium exports are *excluded* from the analysis. This is the processing of bauxite and fits into our concept of "Traditional Exports" and we are interested in nontraditional exports. Aluminum exports are at least 60% of total manufactured exports so their performance would heavily influence the CMS analysis.

to an unfavorable distribution of export markets, a gain in competitiveness, and an unfavorable commodity composition of manufactured exports, in that order of importance. The gain in competitiveness for manufactured exports is in direct contrast to the negative competitiveness effect for the total export performance. In the latter case the competitiveness effect is a relatively more important component of the export performance. The contrasting results suggest that supply considerations are a relatively more important problem in the case of nonmanufactured merchandise exports.

Generally, the performance of manufactured exports in 1970–1979 was superior to the performance of total exports in that period. The actual increase in exports is greater than the hypothetical increase in exports, indicating that Jamaica's manufactured exports gained market share in 1970–1979. The export performance was attributable to overall competitiveness in manufactured exports and a favorable commodity composition of exports. There was an unfavorable distribution of export markets that adversely affected export performance, but this was the least important of the components.

In contrast, the export performance deteriorated in the 1979–1987 period. The actual increase in manufactured exports was negative and significantly less than the hypothetical increase, indicating that Jamaica's manufactured exports lost world market share. The unfavorable distribution of export markets worsened and became the most important component of the export performance. The previously positive competitiveness effect became negative, but was not as important to the export performance as in 1970–1979. The composition of the export basket was unfavorable as the effect became negative, but it remained the second most important of the three components.

In Table 2.16 the top ten items in the RCA vectors for total exports are presented for Jamaica for the years 1970, 1979, and 1987. In Jamaica, between 1970 and 1979, comparative advantage based on RCA indexes was lost in vegetables etc. fresh, simply preserved; tobacco manufactures; other nonmetal mineral manufactures; fruit, preserved, or prepared; fresh fruit, nuts; and chocolate and its products. Revealed comparative advantage was acquired only in essential oil, perfume etc. In the period 1970–1979 Jamaica seems to have had relatively more unfavorable than favorable shifts in the number of products with revealed comparative advantage. This would imply some weakening of the country's export performance.

One can pose the following question: Why does one observe these unfavorable shifts in RCA in Jamaica in the 1970–1979 period? As was the case in Trinidad and Tobago, the export sector in Jamaica is dominated by one primary export—bauxite. In Jamaica bauxite exports were 70.3% of total merchandise exports in 1970, and 71.8% in 1979. The bauxite industry expanded rapidly in the 1960s to around the mid-1970s. Bauxite exports grew at an annual average rate of 11.2% between 1960–1970. Given the dependence of the economy on bauxite exports and the boom in the industry, one could argue that there were similar effects on relative prices and domestic costs in Jamaica, as there were in Trinidad and Tobago, negatively affecting export competitiveness. The CMS results for the 1970–1979 period indicate that the negative competitiveness effect was the most important component of the total export performance. This is consistent with the above analysis of the factors behind the shifts in RCA.

In 1987 Jamaica exhibited revealed comparative advantage in a wider range of products than in 1979. Revealed comparative advantage in the export sector was spread over all product types (i.e. primary products, crops and animal products), moderately capital or skill intensive manufactures, and labor intensive manufactures. Despite the wider range of products with an RCA greater than unity, the CMS results for the 1979–1987 period still point to a negative competitiveness effect and supply considerations are still the most important component of the export performance.

In the 1979–1987 period Jamaica introduced a range of policy measures via IMF programs aimed at correcting the disequilibrium in the balance of payments. Simultaneously the country accessed World Bank Structural Adjustment

**Table 2.16**
**Top Ten Items in RCA Vector**
**for Jamaica—1970, 1979, and 1987[1]**

| JAMAICA | |
|---|---|
| **Commodity Type** | **1970** |
| P | Base Metal Ores, Concentrate (Bauxite) |
| CAP | Vegetables etc. fresh, simply preserved |
| CAP | Spices |
| CAP | Fruit, Preserved, Prepared |
| CAP | Tobacco Manufacturers |
| CAP | Alcoholic Beverages |
| CAP | Fruit, Fresh, Nuts |
| LI | Other non-metal mineral manufacturers* |
| CAP | Chocolate and Products |
| CAP | Sugar and Honey |
| **Commodity Type** | **1979[2]** |
| P | Base Metal Ores, Concentrate (Bauxite) |
| CAP | Spices |
| CAP | Sugar and Honey |
| CAP | Alcoholic Beverages |
| HCSI | Essential Oil, Perfume etc.* |
| CAP | Fruit, Preserves, Prepared |
| **Commodity Type** | **1987** |
| P | Base Metal Ores, Concentrate (Bauxite) |
| CAP | Sugar and Honey |
| CAP | Spices |
| MCSI | Iron, Steel, Universal Plate Sheet* |
| CAP | Cocoa |
| LI | Outer Garments not knit* |
| CAP | Alcoholic Beverages |
| CAP | Vegetables etc. Fresh, Preserved |
| LI | Men's Outerwear, not knit* |
| HCSI | Soaps, Cleaning etc. Preparation* |

**Sources:** Calculated from data taken from the *U.N. Yearbook of International Trade Statistics* and the *U.N. Commodity Trade Statistics*.

**Notes:** [1]Items are listed in descending order (i.e. from highest to lowest indexes in the top ten; [2]There are only six items with an RCA greater than unity. Asterisks indicate manufactured exports.

loans (SALs) that contained policy conditionalities. The development of non-traditional exports, including manufactured exports, was an important objective of these programs. Among the price and nonprice policy-related changes that occurred were devaluations, changes in the exchange rate regime (crawling peg, the auction system and market-based exchange rates) the relaxation of import controls, wage freezes, creation of export processing zones, and new export promotion organizations. It is likely that the new policy regime contributed to the shifts in RCA rankings that one observes in 1987. However, the CMS results do not reflect any positive impact on the supply-side factors as a consequence of the adjustment measures.

The top ten items in the RCA vectors based on manufactured exports are presented in Table 2.17. The results indicate that manufactured exports from Jamaica with an RCA greater than unity are concentrated in labor intensive areas, the most important being the clothing industry. In contrast, Barbados's RCA (based on manufactured exports) is spread across all three types of manufactures with electronic and clothing exports being the major areas. In the case of Trinidad and Tobago, the highly capital or skill intensive manufactured exports appear to be the products in which RCA is strongest; however, there is revealed comparative advantage in some labor intensive areas.

## 2.4 AN ASSESSMENT OF THE RESULTS

A key feature of the results of the CMS and RCA analyses is the importance of supply factors to the Caribbean countries export performance in the 1970–1987 period. The CMS results indicate that in the 1970–1987 period, and particularly in the 1979–1987 subperiod, the competitiveness effect was the most important component of the manufactured export performance in Barbados and Trinidad and Tobago, where it moved from positive to negative, from the 1970–1979 subperiod to the 1979–1987 subperiod, and increased in importance as a component of the manufactured export performance. In the case of Jamaica the competitiveness effect was negative in the 1979–1987 subperiod, but the least important of the components of the manufactured export performance. Notably, the competitiveness effect was positive for the entire 1970–1987 period and was the second most important component of the manufactured export performance.

In the case of the total export performance in Barbados and Jamaica, the competitiveness effect was the most important component in the 1970–1987 period. In Barbados it increased in size and importance from 1970–1979 to 1979–1987. In Trinidad and Tobago the competitiveness effect moved from being negative in the 1970–1979 subperiod to positive in the 1979–1987 subperiod, and increased in relative importance. The reversal in sign is partially attributable to a range of adjustment measures that were introduced in the 1979–1987 subperiod.

The RCA analysis reflects gains and losses in revealed comparative advantage in all three countries. In Jamaica and Trinidad and Tobago in the 1970–1979 subperiod, RCA is lost in more commodities than it is acquired in. A possible explanation is that Dutch disease-type effects adversely affected relative prices

**Table 2.17**
**Top Ten Items in RCA Vector (Manufactured**
**Exports) for Jamaica—1970, 1979, and 1987**

| JAMAICA[1] | |
|---|---|
| **Commodity Type** | **1970** |
| LI | Other non-metal mineral manufacturers |
| HCSI | Pigments, Paints etc. |
| MCSI | Base Metal Household Equipment |
| LI | Gold, Silverware, Jewelry |
| LI | Articles of Paper |
| LI | Articles of Plastic etc. |
| **Commodity Type** | **1979** |
| HCSI | Soaps, Cleaning etc. Preparations |
| LI | Under Garments not knit |
| HCSI | Perfume, Cosmetics etc. |
| HCSI | Pigments, Paints etc. |
| MCSI | Structures and Parts, etc. |
| LI | Other Manufactured Goods |
| **Commodity Type** | **1987** |
| LI | Men's Outerwear, not knit |
| LI | Outer Garments, not knit |
| HCSI | Soaps, Cleaning etc. Preparation |
| LI | Under Garments, not knit |
| LI | Women's Outerwear, not knit |
| HCSI | Perfume, Cosmetics etc. |

**Sources:** Calculated from data taken from the *U.N. Yearbook of International Trade Statistics* and the *U.N. Commodity Trade Statistics*.

**Note:** [1]Jamaica does not have ten items with an RCA greater than one for each year. These are the items with an RCA greater than unity.

and domestic costs in the 1970–1979 subperiod, negatively affecting competitiveness in the export sector. In 1987, in both countries, RCA is acquired in new commodities and there are now at least ten items with an RCA greater than unity. It is suggested that policy responses to balance of payments disequilibrium positively influenced supply factors. However, in the case of Jamaica this is not reflected in the CMS results for the 1979–1987 subperiod.

The lack of export diversification in the export baskets of Trinidad and Tobago and Jamaica is reflected in both the CMS and RCA analysis. In the CMS analysis for Trinidad and Tobago, the commodity composition effect is the most important component of the total export performance in the 1970–1987 period and the 1970–1979 and 1979–1987 subperiods. The effect moves from being positive to negative over the two subperiods. This is indicative of the declining fortunes of the oil industry in the 1979–1987 subperiod. As stated earlier, the RCA results for 1970 and 1979 reflect the effect of the booming oil industry on the rest of the domestic economy.

In Jamaica the weak export performance over the 1970–1987 period and both subperiods is largely explained by the deteriorating export performance of the two major primary exports—bauxite and sugar. Together they account for over 70% of total merchandise exports. In addition, the loss of RCA in a number of commodities in the 1970–1979 subperiod is attributable to the effects on the local economy of the 1960s bauxite boom.

In conclusion, the CMS and RCA techniques are useful tools of descriptive analysis to help paint a detailed picture of a country's export performance in a specific period. The techniques have been applied for the first time to three important CARICOM countries and the results are complementary to each other. The challenge is to develop an economic model that highlights the key variables behind these countries export performance. This will be attempted in a later chapter.

## NOTES

1. Some examples of previous studies that have employed the RCA concept are Balassa (1965; 1977), UNIDO (1982), or Yeats (1985).

2. The CMS analysis is done using current price export data as it was not possible to get detailed constant price data. Hence, one is assuming away differences in price movements across selling countries for specific commodities.

3. I am aware that the coverage of data is not fully consistent across different sources. Often U.S. import data differ from those of exporters. There are differences between the data reported in the *U.N. Yearbook of International Trade Statistics* and the *U.N. Commodity Trade Statistics*. In the case of the former, the totals for commodity groups based on SITC three-digit classifications tend to be higher than those reported in the *U.N. Commodity Trade Statistics*. These differences are quite acute in some years in the period 1968–1987 for Costa Rica. The *U.N. Commodity Trade Statistics* are used as they provide detailed data on the direction of trade of an individual country necessary for CMS analysis.

4. Some of the categorizations appeared questionable (e.g., cement as a labor intensive commodity), but in order to facilitate comparisons with others that use these, no attempt was made to improve them. It should be noted that the categories originally developed by Leamer were based on U.S. data.

5. It was not possible to get data on the number and size of firms that closed their operations in 1987.

6. The deterioration in Trinidad and Tobago's manufactured export performance began to reverse itself after 1988, but this is not the sample period. Anecdotal evidence suggests that some of the "new" capital intensive exports started in the 1970s have significantly improved their performance—notably, methanol, fertilizers, urea, and steel rods. In addition, other areas of manufacturing (e.g., consumer electronics) have begun to penetrate new markets.

7. Since 1987 these industries have continued to expand and by 1990 Central Bank estimates indicate that they account for at least 30% of total exports reducing the economy's dependence on crude oil exports.

## APPENDIX 2.A.1
## DERIVATION OF THE CMS MODEL

We will need the following definitions:

$V_i^{(1)}$ = Value of developing country exports of commodity $i$ in period 1.

$V_i^{(2)}$ = Value of developing country exports of commodity $i$ in period 2.

$V_{ij}$ = Value of developing country exports of commodity $i$ to market $j$.

$r$ = Percentage increase in aggregate world trade from period 1 to period 2.

$r_i$ = Percentage increase in the world trade for commodity $i$ from period 1 to period 2.

$r_{ij}$ = Percentage increase in the world export of commodity $i$ to market $j$ from period 1 to period 2.

From the definition we have:

$$\sum_i \sum_j V_{ij} = \sum_i V_i = V \dots$$

Initially, we may view exports as being completely undifferentiated as to commodity and region of destination. In other words, exports may be seen as a single good destined for a single market. If developing countries maintained their share in this market, then exports would increase by

$$r \sum_i V_i \dots ,$$

and one may write the following identity:

$$V^{(2)} - V^{(1)} \equiv rV + (V^{(2)} - V^{(1)} - rV) \dots \qquad (1)$$

Identity (1) splits the growth in developing country exports into a part associated with the general increase in world exports and an unexplained residual, the competitiveness effect. This is referred to as a "one-level" analysis.

Instead we may argue that exports are in fact quite a diverse set of commodities and what we really have in mind is the world market for a particular commodity class. For the $i^{th}$ commodity we may write an expression analogous to equation (1).

$$V_i^{(2)} - V_i^{(1)} \equiv r_i V_i + (V_i^{(2)} - V_i^{(2)} - r_i V_i )... , \qquad (2)$$

which may be aggregated to

$$V^{(2)} - V^{(1)} \equiv \sum_i r_i V_i + \sum_i (V_i^{(2)} - V_i^{(1)} - r_i V_i^{(1)})$$

$$\equiv (rV ... ) = \sum_i (r-r) V_i + \sum_i (V_i^{(2)} - V_i^{(1)} - r_i V_i^{(1)}). \qquad (3)$$
$$\quad\; (1) \qquad\qquad (2) \qquad\qquad\qquad (3)$$

In identity (3) the growth of developing country exports is attributed to:

1. the general increase in world exports;
2. the commodity composition of developing country exports in Period 1; and
3. an unexplained residual indicating the difference between developing countries actual export increase and the hypothetical increase if developing countries had maintained their share of the exports of each commodity group.

Finally, we may observe that exports are differentiated by destination as well as by commodity type. We have to make allowance for the fact that some countries have easy access to fast growing regions while others are surrounded by slow growing countries. The norm that is used in this case is a constant share of exports of a particular commodity class to a particular region. The identity analogous to (1) and (2) is:

$$V_{ij}^{(2)} - V_{ij}^{(1)} \equiv r_{ij} V_{ij} + (V_{ij}^{(2)} - V_{ij}^{(1)} - r_{ij} V_{ij}^{(1)}) ... , \qquad (4)$$

which when aggregated yields

$$V^{(2)} - V^{(1)} = \sum_i \sum_j r_{ij} V_{ij}^{(1)} + \sum_i \sum_j (V_{ij}^{(2)} - V_{ij}^{(1)} - r_{ij} V_{ij}^{(2)})$$

$$\equiv rV ... + \sum_i (r_j - r) V_i^{(1)} + \sum_i \sum_j (r_{ij} - r_i) V_{ij} \qquad (5)$$
$$\quad\; (1) \qquad\quad (2) \qquad\qquad\qquad (3)$$

$$+ \sum_i \sum_j \underbrace{(V_{ij}^{(2)} - V_{ij}^{(1)} - r_{ij}V_{ij}^{(1)})}_{(4)} \dots \tag{6}$$

Identity (6) attributes the growth in developing country exports to: (1) the general increase in world exports; (2) the commodity composition of developing country exports; (3) the market distribution of developing country exports; and (4) a residual reflecting the difference between the actual export growth and the growth that would have occurred if developing countries had maintained their share of the exports of each commodity to each country.

Note that CMS analysis can be carried out for different levels of aggregation (e.g., groups of countries or individual countries and commodity classes or individual commodities).

## APPENDIX 2.A.2
## COMMODITIES AND MARKETS FOR CMS ANALYSIS

### BARBADOS

a. *Markets*

Trinidad and Tobago

Jamaica

Guyana

United Kingdom

United States of America

Canada

Grenada

St. Vincent

St. Lucia

St. Kitts

Japan

Malaysia

Philippines

Germany, Federal Republic

b. *Commodities*

001—Live Animals

048—Cereals etc. Preparations

054—Fruit, Fresh, Preserved, prepared

061—Sugar and Honey

091—Margarine, Shortening

111—Non-Alcoholic Beverages

112—Alcoholic Beverages

122—Tobacco Manufacturers

273—Stone, Sand and Gravel

332—Petroleum Products

533—Pigments, Paints etc.

541—Medicinal etc. Products

553—Perfume, Cosmetics etc.

554—Soaps, Cleaning etc. Preparations

581—Plastic Materials etc.

591—Pesticides, Disinfectants

599—Miscellaneous Chemical Products

642—Articles of Paper etc.

656—Textile Products etc.

661—Cement, Building Products etc.

691—Structures and Parts

697—Base Metal Household Equipment

698—Metal Manufactures etc.

729—Electrical Machinery

772—Switchgear etc. Parts

776—Transistors Valves etc.

778—Electrical Machinery etc.

821—Furniture

841—Clothing not of Fur

843—Women's Outerwear not Knit

844—Undergarments not Knit

846—Undergarments Knitted

864—Watches and Clocks

891—Sound Recorders, Producers

892—Printed Matter

893—Articles of Plastic etc.

894—Toys, Sporting Goods etc.

897—Gold, Silverware, Jewelry

899—Other Manufactured Goods

## TRINIDAD AND TOBAGO

a. *Markets*

Barbados

Guyana

United States of America

Jamaica

United Kingdom

Canada

Grenada

St. Lucia

Netherlands

Bahamas

St. Vincent

Germany

Venezuela

Sweden

Italy

b. *Commodities*

011—Meat Fresh, Chilled, Frozen

014—Meat Prepared, Preserved etc.

022—Milk and Cream

034—Fish and Preparations

036—Shell Fish Fresh, Frozen

047—Other Cereal Meals, Flour

048—Cereal Preparation etc.

054—Vegetables etc., Fresh, Simply Preserved

056—Vegetables etc., Preserved, Prepared

057—Fruits, Nuts, Fresh, Dried

058—Fruit Preserved, Prepared

062—Sugar and Honey

071—Coffee

072—Cocoa

073—Chocolate and Products

081—Animal Feeding Stuff

091—Margarine, Shortening

098—Food Preparations, etc.

112—Alcoholic Beverages

278—Other Crude Minerals

333—Petroleum (Crude)

334—Petroleum Products

335—Residual Petroleum Products

422—Fixed Vegetable Oil, Nonsoft

512—Hydrocarbons, etc. Derivations

513—Inorganic Elements, Oxides etc.

516—Other Organic Chemicals

522—Inorganic Chemicals

533—Pigments, Paints, etc.

541—Medicinal, Pharmaceutical Products

553—Perfume, Cosmetics etc.

554—Soaps, Cleaning etc. Preparations

561—Fertilizers, Manufactured

581—Plastic Materials etc.

598—Chemicals etc.

629—Rubber Articles

642—Articles of Paper

652—Cotton Fabrics, Woven

661—Cement, Building Products etc.

662—Clay, Refractory Building Products

665—Glassware

673—Iron, Steel Shapes etc.

678—Iron, Steel Tubes, Pipes etc.

691—Structures and Parts etc.

692—Metal Tanks, Boxes etc.

699—Metal Manufactures etc.

723—Civil Engineering Equipment, etc.

727—Food Machinery, Non-Domestic

775—Household-type Equipment, etc.

792—Aircraft etc.

821—Furniture

842—Men's Outerwear not Knit

844—Undergarments not Knit

846—Under garments Knitted

851—Footwear

892—Printed Matter

893—Articles of Plastic etc.

897—Gold, Silverware, Jewelry

899—Other Manufactured Goods

## JAMAICA

a. *Markets*

Trinidad and Tobago

Guyana

Barbados

United States of America

Canada

United Kingdom

Netherlands

Japan

Germany

Sweden

Australia

Venezuela

Ghana

Norway

USSR

Guatemala

Honduras

Panama

Belize

b. *Commodities*

048—Cereal Preparation etc.

051—Fruit Fresh, Nuts

053—Fruit, Preserved, Prepared

054—Vegetables etc. Fresh, Simply Preserved

061—Sugar and Honey

062—Sugar Preparations, Non-chocolate

071—Coffee

073—Chocolate and Products

075—Spices

099—Food Preparations nos.

112—Alcoholic Beverages

122—Tobacco Manufactures

251—Pulp and Waste Paper

287—Base Metal Ores, Concentrate

334—Petroleum Products

533—Pigments, Paints etc.

541—Medicinal, Pharmaceutical Products

551—Essential Oil, Perfume etc.

554—Soaps, Cleaning etc. Preparation

581—Plastic Materials etc.

591—Pesticides, Disinfectants

641—Paper etc. Precut

642—Articles of Paper

652—Cotton Fabrics, Woven

658—Textile Articles etc.

663—Other Non-metal Mineral Manufactures's

674—Iron, Steel Unbound Plate Sheet

684—Aluminum

691—Structures and Parts, nos.Other Organic Chemicals

727—Food Machinery, Non-Domestic

772—Switchgear etc. Parts nos.

773—Electrical Distributing Equipment

775—Household Type Equipment

821—Furniture

842—Men's Outerwear not Knit

843—Women's Outerwear not Knit

844—Undergarments not Knit

845—Outer Garments not Knit

851—Footwear

892—Printed Matter

893—Articles of Plastic etc.

897—Gold, Silverware, Jewelry

899—Other Manufactured Goods

**Source:** Rana (1988) p. 19 (Appendix 2).

**Note:** Rana (1988) converted the original Table in E. Leamer, *Sources of International Comparative Advantage: Theory and Evidence* (Cambridge, Mass.: MIT Press, 1984).

# 3

## "Incentives" and Institutional Support for Exports

In the literature the question of export promotion is closely related to the structure of incentives in an individual country. The NBER (National Bureau of Economic Research) studies [Bhagwati (1978); Krueger (1978)] classified trade strategies for a group of countries using incentive-related classifications.

A significant correlation was found to exist between countries with a strong export performance and a trade-neutral or bias-free incentive structure. The empirical studies of the four most successful Far Eastern economies—Hong Kong, Korea, Taiwan, and Singapore—indicated these four countries were closer to neutrality than to a substantial bias on exports.[1] It is on this basis that an export-promoting trade strategy is defined as one where there are neutral incentives between export promoting (EP) and import substituting (IS) activities.

More formally, the EP strategy is defined as the adoption of an effective exchange rate for the country's exports ($EER_X$), which is approximately equal to that for imports ($EER_M$). Bhagwati suggests that the $EER_X$ would include, for a peso currency country, "not just the pesos earned at parity from a unit of dollar's worth of export, but also any export subsidy, tax credits, and special credits" (1988: 57). Similarly, the EER would add to the parity any existing import duty and import premium resulting from quantitative restrictions (QRs) and any other charges. The following classifications were suggested by Bhagwati (1988):

IS Strategy: $EER_X < EER_M$

$$\text{EP Strategy:} \qquad EER_X \approx EER_M$$
$$\text{Ultra-EP Strategy:} \qquad EER_X > EER_M$$

Bhagwati admits that it is not uncommon, especially among policymakers, to find definitions of the EP strategy referring to both neutral incentives and the ultra-EP strategy. The IS strategy is characterized by antiexport bias and the focus of policy should be to eliminate the antiexport bias creating neutral incentives, thereby fostering export development. In the literature, notably from the World Bank, a variety of policy instruments have been suggested, based on the experience of the four Asian newly industrializing economies (NIEs), that would eliminate or remove the antiexport bias.

The purpose of this chapter is to look at the issue of "incentives," particularly the presence or absence of antiexport bias, in CARICOM countries. In this context the set of incentives that are given to exports is examined. In Section 3.1 a background for the analysis is provided by looking at the range of policy instruments that are suggested in the literature, based on the experience of the four Asian NIEs, for removing antiexport bias and expanding exports. In Section 3.2 the issue of antiexport bias is pursued by examining the behavior of the real effective exchange rates of CARICOM countries over the 1968–1989 period.[2] In Section 3.3 the set of export incentives that have been adopted in Jamaica, Barbados, and Trinidad and Tobago are examined.

## 3.1 POLICIES AIMED AT ACHIEVING NEUTRAL INCENTIVES

Recently the World Bank's official publications have suggested that a necessary precondition for achieving neutral incentives between EP and IS activities is that countries must have "neutral status" [see Yung Whee Rhee (1985); Bhattacharya and Linn (1988)]. Neutral status means that a country must be able to compete with its foreign competitors on an equal footing. Yung Whee Rhee argues that to achieve neutral status requires a duty-free status for all imports used in export production. It must be noted that this places potential exporters on an equal footing with world market competitors, but does not necessarily provide incentives equivalent to those for import substituting activities. The achievement of neutral or bias-free incentives requires neutral status and a complementary set of policies. Two sets of policies are suggested to achieve neutral incentives. First, it is recommended that the average level of protection and its variance be reduced from those levels commonly observed. Second, specific measures in support of exports should be adopted. The rationale for the latter is that "such policies can play a role in *offsetting* disincentives to exports, while distortions introduced by import protection are gradually being r*educed*." [Bhattacharya and Linn (1988: 76).[3] A key point to note is that export promotion measures are only suggested on a transitional basis. The argument is that once the antiexport biases in the trade regime have been removed through reform of the protective system, then special measures designed to put exporters on an equal footing with their international competitors are no longer required.

A variety of instruments of export development have been discussed in the literature based on the East Asian Experience but here we will only list the major instruments of export development.[4]

a. *Realistic Exchange Rates*: Guaranteeing a realistic exchange rate (including compensation for overvaluation) for exporters. This is equivalent to maintaining an equilibrium exchange rate for exporters. This is a highly controversial issue in the literature as it is not entirely clear how one determines a country's equilibrium exchange rate. What can be argued is that east Asian NIEs used the exchange rate as an important tool of export development and adjusted the exchange rate as deemed necessary to enhance the competitiveness of the country's exports. Therefore, in their early years of export development they engaged in "competitive devaluations" aimed at maintaining and/or improving export competitiveness.

b. *Free Input and Output Trade*: An efficient system of indirect tax exemptions or rebates/drawbacks for direct and indirect exporters[5] must be implemented that ensures that exporters access to inputs and trade for their outputs at world market prices.

c. *Ready Access to Export Finance*: Easy and uninterrupted access to preshipment working capital (short-term finance) at competitive rates for both direct and indirect exporters. Invariably this requires special programs of assistance including support for small and medium-sized exporters and the introduction of preshipment export finance guarantees.

d. *Access to Primary and Nontraded Inputs at Undistorted Prices*: The principal objective here is to maintain an undistorted labor market and wage structure. It also includes providing nontraded inputs—notably transport, electricity, telecommunication, and other public services—reliably, and at competitive rates.

e. *Adequate Institutional Infrastructure for Trade*: Bhattacharya and Linn suggest that this covers a wide range of policies, including the "provision of timely and low-cost customs clearance, shipping, and port handling facilities, support for export market information gathering, training and research and development (R&D), and assistance with the development of trading companies and exporters' associations" (1988: 17). It also includes an active role for government in international trade negotiations, ensuring that exporters utilize all privileges provided by preferential trading arrangements.

  f. *Free Trade Zones*: A commonly used instrument to implement the above measures is the provision of free trade zones (FTZs).[6] In the FTZs direct exporters are provided with duty-free access to imported inputs with the necessary physical infrastructure, and often with credit and technical assistance and, in some cases, exemption from some of the country's labor laws. In addition, FTZs are used by developing countries to attract direct foreign investment to export industries.

The above export policy instruments are suggested to developing countries as export development policies to complement the reform of the protective system aimed at removing antiexport bias and stimulating export growth. In Appendix 3.A.1 a more detailed summary of the required set of export incentives and the associated administrative agencies is presented.

## 3.2 "INCENTIVES" AND REAL EFFECTIVE EXCHANGE RATES

In developing countries it is usually quite difficult to develop measures of the effective exchange rate for exports or imports as defined by Bhagwati (1988). The major source of difficulty is obtaining time series data on export subsidies, preferential export loans, fiscal incentives, and the like. There have been some calculations of the effective exchange rate in developing countries and generally these have been used in the estimation of export supply functions [see Donges and Riedel (1977) and Yang (1981)]. In these studies the effective exchange rate is defined to be the official exchange rate plus all export subsidies—direct export subsidies, tax exemptions, preferential export loans, and so forth—minus any export taxes. I found it extremely difficult to obtain or develop time series data on export subsidies and preferential export credits for Caribbean countries. Therefore, I used the real effective exchange rate (REER). The REER measures the domestic price of a country's tradable goods (import substitutes as well as exports) relative to nontradable goods over time. Other things equal, when the real value of a currency rises, other policy instruments must be deployed to preserve external balance. Historically these have more frequently protected against imports than encouraged exports. In the 1970s import protection policies were adopted in ad hoc fashion to protect the balance of payments. Whereas tariffs remained relatively constant in the period, quantitative restrictions (QRs) were frequently used in CARICOM countries to protect domestic producers from foreign competitors. The most common type of QRs was license requirements in combination with negative and/or prohibited lists and/or quotas. The presence of QRs is a source of antiexport bias in the incentive structure. It was not possible to develop time series data to capture these changes in the import regime.

In the CARICOM countries the regime of export incentives remained relatively stable after 1974 with the adoption of the CARICOM harmonization of fiscal incentives to industry. Real currency appreciation has usually meant increasing antiexport bias.

The REER is calculated as the inflation-adjusted weighted average of changes in nominal exchange rates of an individual country's currency, vis-à-vis all countries that are important export markets of the individual country.[7] Following Maciejewski (1983: 505) in computing the REER, it is usually assumed that domestic producers in the importing markets are the main competitors to a country's exports, therefore, trade export weights that reflect the shares of a country's major export markets in total exports are used as weights in computing the REER. Using the arithmetic averaging technique, the following definition of the REER results:

$$REER = 100 * \sum_{i=1}^{n} W_i * [(E_{it}/E_{io}) * (P_{it}/P_{io})],$$

where $W_i$ = the normalized export weight and is defined as:

$$W_i = X_i / \sum_{i=1}^{n} X_i,$$

where:

$X_i$      =      the export of commodity $i$ and, $\sum_{i=1}^{n} W_i = 1$.

$(E_{it}/E_{io})$    =      an index of the price of the $i^{th}$ trading partners currency in terms of the home currency in period $t$ relative to base year 0.

$(P_{it}/P_{io})$    =      the ratio of the price index of the $i^{th}$ trading partner in period t relative to the price index of the home country in period $t$, with the base year being 0.

Note, that in the plots of the real effective exchange rates for CARICOM countries the following notation is used:

REERB    =    real effective exchange rate Barbados

REERJ    =    real effective exchange rate Jamaica

REERTT   =    real effective exchange rate Trinidad and Tobago

Given our definition of the REER using aggregate export weights, an increase means a real depreciation (or an increase in the relative price of tradable) and a decrease implies a real appreciation.

The plots of the REERs for Jamaica, Barbados, and Trinidad and Tobago for the period 1968–1989 are presented in Appendix 3.A.2. The behavior of the REER is analyzed for each individual country attempting as far as possible to explain the variation in the REER in the period. The REERs are related to export performance, and this is discussed in Chapter 5.

### Jamaica

Generally, Jamaica's REER appreciates in the subperiod 1968–1972, but depreciates continuously until 1984, appreciates between 1984–1987, and depreciates again after 1987. The depreciation of the REER in 1977–1984 is indicative of an improvement in the relative price of tradables that should have counteracted the antiexport bias in the incentive structure, but one also observes a lot of variation in Jamaica's REER in the period.

In the subperiod 1968–1977 Jamaica maintained a fixed exchange rate policy with the U.S. dollar and movements in the REER were due to inflation differentials and movements of Third World country currencies against the U.S. dollar. The continuous appreciation after 1971 is indicative of the movement to flexible exchange rates in the industrialized countries and the fluctuations of those currencies against the Jamaican dollar. The U.S. dollar crisis in 1971 and the oil price shock of 1973 continued to have a negative impact on the performance of Jamaica's economy. The economy fell into a recession from which it never fully recovered. To respond to the external shocks, expenditure controls were introduced, taxes were increased, credit limits were imposed, some import restrictions were implemented, and foreign exchange purchases were controlled.

After 1974 the Manley government moved decidedly to a policy of "democratic socialism." There was fiscal expansion and an attempt at the socialization of production. There was nationalization in all sectors of the economy and state ownership significantly increased.

To finance the new social programs of the government, which included wage increases in the public sector, the government planned to use the tax receipts from the bauxite levy that was introduced in 1974. The combination of excessive monetary and fiscal expansion with adverse terms of trade movements resulted in severe foreign exchange losses, that in turn lead to a fundamental disequilibrium in the balance of payments, inducing a lot of uncertainty about the level of the nominal exchange rate.

Serious balance of payments problems in 1977 induced Jamaica to seek a standby agreement with the International Monetary Fund (IMF). Since 1977 Jamaica has continued to have a series of programs with the IMF and this has led to the introduction of a variety of exchange rate regimes accompanied by devaluation. The following is a summary of exchange rate changes in Jamaica since 1977:

1. April, 1977: A dual exchange rate system was agreed upon with the IMF with the existing US$1.10/J$1 rate for a list of "essential imports" and bauxite/aluminina valuation and a rate of US$0.80/J$1 for all other transactions.

2. May 1978: The dual rate was abandoned and an exchange rate "crawl" was introduced that allowed for monthly devaluations of $1\frac{1}{2}\%$.

3. January 1983: The Jamaican authorities allowed the banking system to determine the rates for the buying and selling of currency, apart from official transactions, bauxite pricing and a number of designated imports, for which the official exchange rate remained fixed.

4. November 1983: The exchange rates were unified by devaluing the official rate from J$1.78/US$1 to J$3.15. The authorities allowed the exchange rate to fluctuate J$0.15 on either side of this midrate.

5. In 1984 an auction system was introduced and twice weekly foreign exchange auctions were conducted by the Central Bank of Jamaica. Worrell (1987) estimated that the exchange rate depreciated at an average rate of 10.5% per quarter between December 1983 and March 1985.

6. Since 1984 the most significant developments have been the use of an interbank float and finally the move to exchange rate liberalization.

This combination of exchange rate regimes accompanied by a series of devaluations was largely responsible for the sharp depreciation of the REER for Jamaica in the subperiod 1977–1985. Worrell argued that Jamaica pursued an "adventurous exchange rate policy" (1987: 127) that led to a lot of fluctuations in the nominal exchange rate, which did not necessarily assist exporters. Some analysts argue that under certain conditions devaluation can counteract antiexport bias and improve export performance, but there must be stability to generate an export response [Worrell (1987); UNCTAD (1989)].

The appreciation of the REER between 1985–1987 is largely due to the appreciation of the U.S. dollar relative to European currencies. This trend in the dollar started in the early 1980s, but was particularly noticeable after 1984 and continued through until 1987 when there was a sharp depreciation. The depreciation of the U.S. dollar and the continued depreciation of the Jamaican dollar as determined by the auction system combined to lead to a sharp depreciation of the REER after 1987.

In summary, persistent balance of payments problems have forced Jamaica to adopt a variety of programs with the IMF since 1977. These programs have lead to the adoption of a variety of exchange rate regimes that have been accompanied by devaluations. The continuous devaluation of the Jamaican dollar has been largely responsible for a depreciation of the REER since 1977. Between 1985–1987 there was a temporary appreciation of the U.S. dollar but the REER depreciated once again after 1987.

## Trinidad and Tobago

In Trinidad and Tobago the REER appreciated in 1968–1984, particularly in the 1976–1982 subperiod. In the period 1968–1984 Trinidad and Tobago maintained a fixed exchange rate regime and was pegged to the U.S. dollar. The appreciation of the REER was largely due to relatively higher inflation rates than its major trading partners. This was particularly true in the 1976–1982 subperiod when Dutch disease–type effects stimulated increased inflation. Worrell (1987) argues that the demand for nontradables exceeded capacity and inflation gained momentum. In every year between 1976–1979 these price increases were in double digits. The sharp increase in aggregate expenditure put considerable stress on the country's infrastructure, particularly at Port of Spain in the 1970s. Transportation bottlenecks created artificial shortages, inducing increases in the retail prices of imported goods that resulted in higher inflation.

The boom in the petroleum sector began to taper off in 1982 but aggregate expenditures continued to expand due to large wage increases in the public and private sector. In 1981 sugar workers wages were increased by 94% for the 1980–1982 period. This was an effort to catch up with increases in wages for oilfield workers (42% for 1981–1983), government (62–86% 1981–1983), and transport workers (48% 1980–1982). The continued growth in expenditure and the increased cost of labor continued to encourage inflation appreciating the REER.

In 1985 government introduced expenditure cuts, a wage freeze, exchange controls, and a devaluation of the Trinidad and Tobago dollar from US$1/TT$2.40 to US$1/TT$3.60 to improve the fiscal situation and the balance of payments. The devaluation led to a sharp depreciation of the REER in 1985. In 1985–1986 the REER appreciated slightly resulting from the appreciation of the U.S. dollar vis-à-vis European currencies. After 1986 Trinidad and Tobago entered into a standby agreement with the IMF that included a further devaluation from US$1/TT$3.60 to US$1/TT$4.25, resulting in yet another depreciation of the REER.

In short, Dutch disease–type effects in 1976–1982 stimulated substantial wage increases and rising aggregate expenditures leading to double digit inflation, an erosion of international competitiveness and a steady appreciation of the REER. Since 1985 Trinidad has had to introduce austerity measures to protect the balance of payments, including two devaluations of the exchange rate that have depreciated the REER.

## Barbados

There has been a continuous appreciation of the REER (except for 1986) in the period 1968–1989. The macroeconomic environment displayed a higher degree of stability, except for 1973–1974 and 1981–1983, than any of the other three major CARICOM economies. The environment has been characterized by growth, balance of payments stability, low inflation, and prudent financial management.

If one examines the plot for Barbados's REER, there appears to be a structural break in 1976. From 1968–1976 the REER appreciated sharply largely due to international influences. Between 1968–1975 Barbados pegged its exchange rate to the sterling and that link was maintained until July 1975, when the parity for the Barbados dollar was redefined in terms of U.S. dollars. In the subperiod there was the evolution of managed floating international exchange rates and Barbados's REER was affected by the sterling's appreciations vis-à-vis other currencies. In the subperiod 1976–1983 the REER is relatively stable with a slight depreciation in 1980. The subperiod 1976–1983 is characterized as a period of growth and balance of payments stability in the Barbadian economy after the downturn in 1973–1974 following the oil crisis. Between 1983–1986 the REER appreciated sharply once again, largely due to the appreciation of the U.S. dollar (Barbados's major trading partner) vis-à-vis European currencies. The depreciation of the U.S. dollar in 1986 led to a depreciation of the REER but it began to appreciate after 1987 when the U.S. dollar reversed its depreciation.

In short, the behavior of Barbados's REER in the period 1968–1989 was largely influenced by international circumstances. Initially, Barbados pegged its currency to the sterling (until 1975) and the movement to managed international floating exchange rates after 1971 influenced appreciation of major currencies against the sterling. After 1983 the appreciation of the U.S. dollar led to further appreciation of the REER.

In summary, there was noticeable variation in the real effective exchange rates of Jamaica and Trinidad and Tobago. Macroeconomic instability and movements in international exchange rates can be categorized as the major influences on the behavior of these countries REERs. In contrast, Barbados's real effective exchange rate appreciated continuously in the period 1968–1989. The macroeconomic environment was generally stable throughout the period. The movements in Barbados's REER were attributable to changes in international exchange rates. Having looked at the behavior of the REERs and analyzed the stability of the incentives structure, we now look at the export development policies that were introduced to promote exports.

## 3.3  INSTRUMENTS OF EXPORT DEVELOPMENT POLICY IN CARICOM COUNTRIES

In the immediate years after independence most CARICOM countries adopted the Lewis strategy of "Industrialization by Invitation" [see Lewis (1950)]. Lewis essentially argued that these countries were short of capital and entrepreneurial skills and should use foreign investment as a means of acquiring both of these necessary resources. The relatively low cost of labor should be complemented by a range of fiscal incentives that would encourage foreign firms to locate particularly in the manufacturing sector in CARICOM countries. Lewis anticipated that after an initial period of learning, CARICOM producers would be able to start their own enterprises and develop the industrial base of these countries, particularly in manufactured exports.

Guided by the Lewis strategy, the CARICOM territories passed fiscal incentive legislation and built industrial estates to provide factory space to encourage foreign investors. The formation of the CARICOM integration movement in 1974 was supposed to lead to a common approach to the development of industry. Although there has been some harmonization, there still remains a lot of divergence among national policies.

### Fiscal Incentives

Under the CARICOM treaty, promotion of industry has been implemented under two distinct arrangements. The trade regime has provided protection from extraregional competition through tariffs [notably the Common External Tariff (CET)] and quantitative restrictions. There is another set of arrangements that has been established and aimed at promoting industry. These include: (1) the Agreement on the Harmonization of Fiscal Incentives to Industry (HFII), and (2) the Industrial Allocation Scheme for the OECS states.[9] The HFII was designed to encourage new manufacturing enterprises and reduce the competition between CARICOM states for foreign investment.

The incentives to industry granted under the scheme are summarized in Table 3.1. Among the key instruments of the HFII are the tax holidays on profits and the duty-free status accorded to approved enterprises. A World Bank (1990b) study states that from a sample of firms that were interviewed, the duty-free status was deemed to be the most valuable of the incentives. The tax holidays

**Table 3.1**
**Fiscal Incentives under Harmonization Scheme**

| Type of Incentive | Duration (Number of Years) | | |
|---|---|---|---|
| 1. Profit tax holiday: | MDCs[1] | Barbados | LDCs[2] |
| •if 100% of sales are exported extra-regionally | 10 | 10 | 15 |
| •if the local value added exceeds 50% of total sales | 9 | 10 | 15 |
| •if the local value added is between 25% and 49% | 7 | 8 | 12 |
| •if the local value added is between 10% and 24% | 5 | 6 | 10 |
| •if the industry is highly capital intensive: for LDCs initial investment exceeds EC$25 million; for MDCs EC$50 million. | 10 | 10 | 15 |
| 2. Tariff exemptions | for the duration of the above tax holiday, inputs, machinery and spare parts can be imported duty-free; all materials and equipment for new factories can be imported duty-free | | |
| 3. Export allowance for extraregional exports after expiration of tax holiday | | | |
| •if export profits exceed 61% of total | •tax relief of 50% for up to 5 years | | |
| •between 41% and 61% of total profits | •tax relief of 45% for up to 5 years | | |
| •between 21% and 41% of total profits | •tax relief of 35% for up to 5 years | | |
| •between 10% and 21% of total profits | | | |
| 4. Divided payments | for the duration of the above tax holiday dividends paid to shareholders are tax exempt | | |
| 5. Loss carry-forward | can carry forward losses for up to 5 years after the tax holiday expires | | |
| 6. Depreciation allowance | after the tax holiday expires, a deduction of up to 20% on any capital expenditure incurred | | |

**Sources:** World Bank (1990b); Industrial Development Corporations in Barbados and Trinidad and Tobago.

**Notes:** [1]CARICOM MDCs are Jamaica, Barbados, Guyana, Trinidad and Tobago, Bahamas, and Belize; [2]CARICOM LDCs are Grenada, St. Lucia, St. Vincent, Dominica, St. Kitts/Nevis, Antigua, and Montserrat.

were considered to be less important since profitable firms would continue to be profitable without tax exemptions, and firms incurring losses are not taxed.

Incentives are not freely available to all firms. They are restricted to only approved products and approved producers. A list of thirty-five products, most

## Table 3.2
## Fiscal and Nonfiscal Incentives

| | Fiscal Incentives | Countries | Description of Policy |
|---|---|---|---|
| 1. | Harmonization of Fiscal Incentives to Industry | All except Guyana | Tax holidays & duty-free inputs for specified time period for approved firms. |
| 2. | International Business Corporations Act | Antigua, Montserrat | Tax-free holidays and duty exemptions from foreign firms; exemptions from foreign exchange controls and levies. |
| 3. | Double Taxation Agreement | All Except St. Lucia and Antigua | Agreement to prevent double taxation of income earned in CARICOM countries. |
| 4. | Free Trade Zone | Jamaica, St. Lucia | For exporting firms, exemption from duties. In Jamaica, automatic tax holidays for unlimited period, in St. Lucia, apply under fiscal incentives act. |
| 5. | Export Incentives not covered by (1) | Jamaica, Guyana, St. Vincent, Belize, Trinidad & Tobago, Barbados | Tax reductions and import, consumption duty exemptions, incentives vary. |
| 6. | Hotel Aids Ordinance | All | Tax and duty exemptions not harmonized across states. |
| 7. | Modernization of Industry Program | Jamaica | Approved firms receive reduction on import duties and assistance for modernization. |
| 8. | Investment Allowance | Trinidad & Tobago, Barbados, Dominica, St. Vincent, St. Lucia | Tax deductions for expenditure on plant and machinery. |
| 9. | Factory Construction | Jamaica, Barbados, Dominica | Tax relief on operating income from leasing of factory or profits from sale of factory. |
| 10. | Bauxite and Alumina Encouragement | Jamaica | 5-10 year exemption from customs duty on imports and machinery. |
| 11. | Locational Incentive | Belize, Trinidad & Tobago, Jamaica | Tax concessions for firms locating in designated areas. |
| 12. | Other Fiscal Incentives not covered by (1) | St. Lucia, Trinidad & Tobago, Grenada, St. Vincent | Incentives for small scale sector (St. Lucia); duty free import of machinery (Trinidad & Tobago, Grenada), negative listing (Trinidad & Tobago). |
| **Other Incentives** | | | |
| 13. | Training of Workers | All | Special wage reduction government-sponsored training programs, variable across CARICOM. |
| 14. | Industrial Estates | All | Factory shells provided at low rental rates, variable across CARICOM. |

**Sources:** World Bank (1990b); Industrial Development Corporation in Barbados and Trinidad and Tobago.

of them final consumer goods such as beer, are explicitly excluded from qualifying as approved products for production in the most developed CARICOM countries (i.e., Jamaica, Guyana, Trinidad and Tobago, and Barbados).

In addition to the fiscal incentives agreement, CARICOM countries also provide a range of other incentives—export incentives, investment allowances, worker training programs, and subsidized rentals on industrial estates. Table 3.2 presents a summary of the range of fiscal and nonfiscal incentives that are provided by individual CARICOM countries.

These additional policies are not harmonized among member states, as can be seen from Table 3.2.[10] An important element of the national policies is that in Jamaica, Guyana, Trinidad and Tobago, Barbados, Belize, and St. Vincent the export incentives permit tax and duty reductions for all exporting firms, while the HFII only permits limited tax relief on exports for approved firms after the expiration of the tax holiday. In addition, in a number of member countries fiscal incentives (mainly duty-free imports of equipment) are granted to firms on an ad hoc basis; specifically, those that do not qualify under HFII.

The existence of additional nonharmonized incentives has undermined the attractiveness and influence of HFII on industrial development in CARICOM. The harmonized scheme must be thoroughly evaluated to assess its usefulness to either introduce revisions or remove the system completely. An important consideration should be the fundamental policy changes that are occurring in CARICOM countries pursuing IMF/World Bank structural adjustment programs (SAPs), notably Jamaica, Guyana, Trinidad and Tobago, and to a lesser extent, Barbados. The SAPS advocate a fundamental shift in policy away from governmental policy interventions, like fiscal incentives, to a greater reliance on market forces. The emphasis of these programs is on the liberalization of markets, particularly factor, product, credit, and foreign exchange markets. A developmental strategy that focuses on economic liberalization does not see fiscal incentives as an integral part of the strategy. Rather, governmental policy interventions are seen as *transitional* policies to be pursued until the process of market-oriented policy reforms is completed. In this context, CARICOM's HFII must be evaluated to determine its usefulness in the long-run strategy of the regional integration movement.

In summary, a wide range of fiscal incentives is offered by CARICOM countries to firms involved in manufacturing. The set of policies offered by HFII and individual national policies provides for duty-free status for imported inputs and significant tax reductions for exporting firms. This is consistent with the key instrument required for "neutral status" as suggested by Yung Whee Rhee (1985) and discussed earlier on. As argued, this is an important element in export development policies aimed at counteracting antiexport bias.

## The Role of the Exchange Rate

The exchange rate has not been used as a deliberate part of government policies toward expanding exports. The exchange rate adjustments that have occurred have been associated with demand management policies. One of the secondary objectives of the devaluations in Jamaica, Guyana, and Trinidad and Tobago has been to stimulate export expansion, but unlike east Asian NIEs, the exchange rate adjustments were not part of an overall package of incentives designed to enhance export competitiveness.

Trinidad and Tobago attempted to manage a dual exchange rate system after its first devaluation of the currency in 1985. The "old" exchange rate was maintained mainly for exporters. The "new" exchange rate was applied to a wide range of imports to reduce expenditure on imports, particularly nonessentials. The dual exchange rate system was abandoned due to a variety of administrative problems and the rate was then unified. It was felt that the serious administrative bottlenecks created by the management of the dual rate was seriously hurting exports. In 1977 Jamaica introduced dual exchange rates for the Jamaican dollar in the context of a IMF supported adjusted program. The rates were eventually unified and the dual rate scheme abandoned in 1978.

All CARICOM countries have imposed limits on foreign exchange transactions through exchange control regimes. Only in Jamaica (from 1971), Guyana (from 1973), and Trinidad and Tobago (from 1982) have these exchange controls been relied upon to control spending. These measures were introduced to reduce foreign exchange outflows and are not related to export development policies. It is difficult to determine whether they adversely affected exporters, but in most cases exporters were given privileged status in the processing of their foreign exchange applications. In Trinidad and Tobago in 1988, exporters who exported 75% of the value of their imports were allowed to access foreign exchange without approval from the Central Bank. Therefore, these exporters faced an exchange control free regime for foreign exchange.[11] Finally, Barbados's exchange control regime and those of the smaller OECS countries are generally considered to be fairly liberal and not a hindrance to exporters.

The experience of CARICOM countries with exchange rate adjustment or devaluation points adds to the importance of exchange rate stability in improving exports and overall macroeconomic performance. The stability of the structure of economic incentives, anchored by a stable exchange rate, is critical to improving investor confidence and stimulating private investment, particularly in the tradable sector. The importance of exchange rate stability does not imply that there should not be any devaluation. Rather, it simply means that devaluation must not be frequent and must be implemented only if the stock of a country's foreign exchange has been completely exhausted and the nominal exchange rate cannot be defended.

In summary, exchange rate policy has not been adopted as part of a package of export promotion policies as was observed in the case of the east Asian NIEs. Devaluations were generally part of IMF stabilization programs aimed at correcting domestic and foreign imbalances.

## Export Processing Zones (EPZs)

Only two members of CARICOM, Jamaica and St. Lucia, currently operate EPZs. However, other CARICOM members, such as Trinidad and Tobago, have recently opened EPZs to encourage manufactured exports.

The EPZs in Jamaica at Kingston and Montego Bay are by far the most developed in the CARICOM area. To operate in the EPZs, a prospective firm is reviewed by the Kingston Free Zone Company Limited. A number of factors are considered before a firm is admitted to the EPZ. These include:

1. The operation must be undertaken by a company incorporated or registered in Jamaica.
2. Production must be for sale outside of Jamaica (i.e., exports).
3. Other factors taken into consideration in respect of an application to operate in the free zone include:
   a. Level and nature of the capital investment
   b. Employment potential
   c. Volume of export sales
   d. Use of local raw materials

Companies operating in the free zone are guaranteed generous incentives, in perpetuity, under the terms of the Jamaica Export Free Zones Act, which regulates activities on the EPZ.

The incentives offered apply to taxation, customs, duty exemptions, and the repatriation of profits. In addition, firms in the EPZs are given priority in all administrative dealings with government ministries and specialized agencies. The incentives offered are:

*a. Tax Exemptions*
- 100% tax holiday on profits

*b. Customs Procedures*
- Waiving of import licensing requirements
- Minimal customs formalities

*c. Duty Exemption*

- No duty is levied on capital goods, consumer goods, raw material, or imports for the construction, extension or repair of Free Zone—including office equipment.

*d. Profit Repatriation*

- There are no restrictions on the repatriation of profits by companies operating in the Zone.
- Client companies are permitted to operate foreign currency accounts in accordance with the Exchange Control Regulations of the Bank of Jamaica.

*e. Work Permits*

- Work permit applications are exempt from the normal taxation.

The above incentives are offered at both the Kingston and Montego Bay EPZs. In the case of the Montego Bay EPZ, two types of activities are encouraged that were not initially accommodated in the Kingston EPZ—distribution and information processing services. The Montego Bay EPZ is seeking to encourage companies to relocate their distribution and warehousing facilities in the EPZ. At the EPZ one can import goods in bulk duty-free, store them, and process them for dispatch to customers worldwide. Processing includes unpackaging, repackaging, purifying, blending, refining, breaking of bulk products, and product consolidation. In addition, goods may be sold duty-free from the Montego Bay EPZ into local bonded warehouses.

Offshore information processing services are also being actively encouraged at the Montego Bay EPZ. A big boost to the industry was the establishment of the Caribbean's first teleport: Jamaica Digiport International (JDI). JDI is a joint venture between American Telegraph and Telephone (AT&T), Cable and Wireless, and Telecommunications of Jamaica (TOJ). The information services industry has grown significantly since its start in 1983. The number of Jamaica-based companies providing export information services has grown from five in 1983 to forty in 1990, and in 1990 they employed over 2,000 individuals.

The EPZs have been an important feature of Jamaica's export development policies and their success has stimulated other CARICOM countries to introduce EPZs as part of their export promotion policies. An obvious question is whether the EPZs have made a significant contribution to the development of exports.[12] In 1985 Jamaica's EPZ exports were 12% of total manufactured exports and increased to 25% of total manufactured exports in 1988. In Jamaica, the EPZs have contributed to the rapid development of the textile industry in the 1980s. The growth of nontraditional exports has been in large part fueled by garment exports from the zone. Exports at the Kingston EPZ have increased at an annual average rate of 6% between 1985–1989. Garment exports were on average 60% of the total exports at the Kingston EPZ between 1985–1989. In short, the data indicate that the EPZ has been successful in encouraging the development of nontraditional exports in Jamaica.[13] It is also important to note that most of the firms operating at the Kingston EPZ are foreign-owned. The data in Table 3.3 are indicative of this.

In Jamaica the relative success of EPZs has seriously undermined the effectiveness of the HFII legislation as a mechanism for promoting investment, industry, and exports. The EPZ model for promoting investment and industry is an alternative to harmonized incentives. CARICOM countries need to decide whether a regional agreement on EPZs will replace harmonized incentives, or whether EPZ legislation makes a regional agreement on harmonized incentives ineffective. Mauritius is a small developing country similar to CARICOM countries and the EPZ model has been implemented there with a great degree of success.

In summary, the Kingston EPZ has been successful in developing nontraditional exports and encouraging foreign investment in manufactured exports.

## Trade Financing

Easy and automatic access to preshipment financing at concessional rates is cited by some authors as an important ingredient in the rapid development of exports in east Asian NIEs [see Rhee, Ross-Larson, and Pursell (1984)]. Export financing arrangements vary across the major CARICOM countries with the most advanced facilities available in Jamaica.

Jamaica created the National Export-Import Bank (EX-IM) in 1986.[14] It is owned jointly by the government of Jamaica and the Bank of Jamaica. The bank was established to provide institutional support to industry with particular

| Table 3.3 Firms Operating at the Kingston EPZ (1989) | | |
|---|---|---|
| **Type of Industry** | **No. of Firms** | **Country of Origin** |
| Garment | 4 | Hong Kong |
| Garment | 4 | U.S.A. |
| Garment | 1 | India |
| Electronics | 1 | Canada |
| Food | 1 | U.S.A. |
| Ethanol | 1 | U.S.A. |
| Warehousing Distribution | 1 | Hungary |
| Animal Food | 1 | U.S.A. |

**Source:** Kingston Free Zone Company Limited.

emphasis on the nontraditional export sector and focuses on supporting credits such as:

1. Short- to medium-term credits to manufacturing and nontraditional agricultural projects, for the acquisition of raw materials, machinery spare parts, intermediate goods, and capital goods.

2. Short- to medium-term credits that generate foreign exchange earnings for the country.

The EX-IM Bank offers the following facilities:

a. Export credit insurance

b. Lines of credit

c. The Export Development Fund (EDF)

d. Preshipment and postshipment facilities (BEGF)

e. The Export Credit Facilities (ECF)

The preshipment financing facility is designed to assist by making advances to an exporter, in relation to the exporters' projections and/or order funds, for the purchase of local raw materials for conversion into finished goods for export and the domestic purchase of finished goods by trading companies. Financing is up to 65% of the FOB value of an order or export projections for a period of ninety days.

There is also the Bankers Export Guarantee Facility (BEGF). The BEGF is a discounting mechanism that allows an exporter to obtain financing equivalent to 80% of the CIF (cost, insurance, and freight) value of a shipment already made upon presentation to the bank of documentary proof evidencing such a shipment. The financing will be for a period of 180 days from the date of shipment. The EX-IM Bank states that the purpose of the facility is to assist and encourage the export of Jamaican manufactured goods by ensuring the continued availability of working capital at a preferred rate of interest.

Finally, there is the Export Credit Facility, which is a discounting mechanism that allows an exporter to obtain financing up to 65% of the FOB value of an export order for a period of ninety days or the equivalent of 80% of the CIF value of a shipment already made. The exporter must present to his or her commercial bank documentary proof evidencing such shipment for a period of 180 days from the date of shipment.

In Trinidad and Tobago export financing facilities are administered by the state-owned Trinidad and Tobago Export Credit Insurance Company Limited (EXICO), a subsidiary of the Trinidad and Tobago Export Development Corporation. The financing facilities provided by EXICO are:

1. Export credit insurance

2. Pre- and postshipment credit guarantees

3. Rediscounting facilities at concessionary rates

Barbados offers a similar set of arrangements but these are administered by the Central Bank of Barbados.

Yung Whee Rhee argues that the experience of the east Asian NIEs demonstrates that "developing countries need smooth running export trade financing systems to support outward-oriented development strategies" (1989). The major CARICOM economies do have export financing arrangements. The issue is whether they are adequate to meet exporters needs and are managed efficiently. The available evidence is patchy at best. In Jamaica officials at the Jamaican Export Promotion Organization (JAMPRO) state that exporters (notably manufacturers) complain that short-term working capital financing is insufficient and that below market interest rates of 15% are still too high. Exporters suggest that the necessary financing arrangements are in place. It is the need for increased working capital financing at more concessionary interest rates that is felt to be the major problem with Jamaica's system of export financing. It is difficult to determine what the exporters' major complaints with the export financing arrangements in Barbados and Trinidad and Tobago are. In the latter case exporters were mainly concerned with reducing the bureaucratic delays they meet when dealing with the government institutions.

## Institutional Support for Exporters: Export Promotion Organizations

Many developing countries have established Export Promotion Organizations (EPOs) to assist the development of nontraditional exports. EPOs in developing countries are usually public sector organizations that offer a variety of services, such as promotional support and other assistance (free of charge) to export marketing, financial schemes administration, policy advice, and representing exporters' needs to the government and the government to the exporters.

In the CARICOM countries EPOs have been established and provide a similar range of services to those described above. Recent research [Keesing and Lall (1988); Keesing (1988)] has found that the successful EPOs in the east Asian NIEs have not functioned like those in most developing countries (including the CARICOM countries). An important distinction is that EPOs in the east Asian NIEs were only established after these countries had attained much experience and success in manufactured exports for many years (e.g., the impressive Trade and Development Board in Singapore was opened in 1983). In developing countries EPOs are usually started at the onset of the adoption of an export promotion strategy.

Research done at the World Bank [Keesing (1988)] indicates that in the early years of export promotion, firms in the east Asian NIEs benefited tremendously from the knowledge they gained from first buyers. Buyers' help was indispensable in showing and teaching potential manufacturers what is required and how to put together the entire package exactly as required. After meeting a succession of orders for the first buyer or buyers, the manufacturing firm becomes "familiar with the stringent quality requirements of export markets, with some product designs and with the production adjustments, packaging, packing and shipping arrangements and management tasks involved" (Keesing and Lall 1988: 9). Eventually the manufacturing firm acquires enough know-how to make it attractive to other buyers. Another part of the learning process that goes on as the firm deals with new buyers is the skill of how to present the firm to buyers emphasizing its experience, management, and production capacity.

On the basis of this it is suggested that in the early years of export promotion EPOs should focus almost exclusively on providing an effective support program of consultancy assistance, complemented by training or design assistance or whatever else is needed. The aim of the program is to improve the export capabilities of firms with the capacity and motivation to export and then help them to market these capabilities. Keesing and Lall argue that the "export consultants" should teach the enterprises so that they become attractive to early buyers or to buyers beyond the early ones. By teaching them much that they would otherwise have to learn from buyers, "this assistance accelerates their learning processes, gives them improved export capabilities, and helps them to move forward quickly to profitable export relationships" (1988: 22).

The focus of the EPOs in the major CARICOM countries—the Barbados Export Promotion Corporation (BEPC); Trinidad and Tobago Export Development Corporation (TTEDC), and the Jamaica National Export Corporation (JAMPRO)—has been on providing the following services (consistent with other developing countries):[15]

   a. *Trade Information Service*: To provide exporters with vital up-to-date information and statistics on overseas markets.

   b. *Market Research*: To provide exporters with detailed research on key overseas markets especially in CARICOM, Europe, and North America.

   c. *Trade Missions and Exhibitions*: To help exporters promote and sell overseas mainly to attend trade fairs.[16]

   d. *Technical Assistance*: To supply advice on key areas affecting export performance (e.g., design, costing and pricing, production management).

   e. *Export Awards*: To recognize and reward outstanding export performance.

One could argue that the activities of the EPOs in the major CARICOM economies are too widespread and should be more narrowly focused in the area of export consultancy advice as mentioned earlier. One suspects that in trying to provide such a wide range of services none of them is done efficiently and increased specialization should be encouraged. Export consultancy advice would provide useful assistance to promising exporting firms and help to build a cadre of successful exporting firms in the individual countries. Ultimately the challenge is for exporting firms to become sufficiently developed so that the export consultancy advice is no longer needed and the EPO can concentrate on providing assistance in overseas promotion.

In conclusion, the development of exports requires the removal of antiexport bias in the incentive structure and the creation of neutral incentives or a proexport incentive structure. It is suggested by some researchers (mainly from the World Bank) that export development policies be introduced simultaneously with tariff reform to counteract the antiexport bias in the trade regime. The experience of the successful east Asian NIEs suggests that the export development policies do encourage the expansion of exports. Research [Yung Whee Rhee (1985); Bhattacharya and Linn (1988)] has distilled the key export development policies adopted by the east Asian NIEs and suggested these as a set of export development policies appropriate for developing countries.

CARICOM countries have adopted a set of export development policies aimed at encouraging the growth of nontraditional exports. These policies are limited only to the extent consistent with the policy framework derived from the experience of the successful east Asian NIEs. Furthermore, the weak export performance over the last two decades suggests the need for changes in the present set of export development policies to enhance the attractiveness of exports. Important changes need to be made to the fiscal incentives, export financing arrangements, forms of institutional support, and the development of EPZs. However, the most important policy objective must be the maintenance of a stable macroeconomic policy environment to further the development of exports.

## NOTES

1. This is a controversial issue in the literature. Robert Wade (1988) argues that in the aggregate trade, regimes in Korea and Taiwan are characterized by neutral incentives. However, at a more disaggregated level there is a wide dispersion of incentives with a strong bias in favor of specific industries.

2. As will be explained later these are not defined in the sense in which Bhagwati (1988) did or as they were done in the 1978 NBER project on trade regimes.

3. Another rationale for export development policies is that there are externalities in export marketing, information gathering, and technology development that require government intervention.

4. It should be noted that a lot of the instruments of export development that are discussed are really focused on the development of manufactured exports, not service exports (e.g., data processing, telemarketing, etc.) or "other" nontraditional exports (e.g., cut flowers).

5. These are defined as firms whose outputs are used as inputs in the production of exports.

6. Outside of the East Asian NIEs, Mauritius is cited as a "success" story in the use of FTZs for the development of manufactured exports, particularly textile and clothing exports.

7. A variety of weights can be used in calculating the REER. Some of these are used in calculating the REER for Caribbean countries in a later chapter.

8. This is done to maintain consistency with the definitions that are used in the export supply regressions in Chapter 5.

9. These are the smaller member states of CARICOM that formed a subregional integration movement—The Organisation of Eastern Caribbean States. It is comprised of Grenada, St. Vincent, St. Lucia, Dominica, St. Kitts and Nevis, Antigua, and Montserrat.

10. The variance in the additional incentives provided by CARICOM member states contradicts one of the aims of HFII, that is, reducing rivalry among individual countries for foreign investment.

11. Interviews with some manufacturers in Trinidad and Tobago indicate that the foreign exchange accounts are a strong incentive to get involved in exports.

12. An important factor to be considered in analyzing the performance of an EPZ is the net foreign exchange contribution of firms in the EPZ. In Jamaica the import content of most of the exports in the EPZs, such as electronic and garment assembly, is generally high. The following data provide some insight into the net foreign exchange contribution of firms at the Kingston free zone. ($US million).

|         | 1985 | 1986 | 1987 | 1988 |
|---------|------|------|------|------|
| Exports | 43.5 | 69.7 | 97.7 | 101.4 |
| Imports | 39.9 | 55.3 | 73.8 | 62.4 |
| Balance | 3.4  | 14.4 | 23.9 | 39 |

**Source:** Kingston Free Zone Company Limited.

13. Recently officials at the Kingston Free Zone Company Ltd. have admitted that there is some dissatisfaction among the firms at the EPZ. The main problems cited are the unionization of workers and utility stoppages.

14. The Bank absorbed all of the programs previously administered by the Jamaica Export Credit Insurance Corporation (JECIC).

15. I visited these three EPOs and these findings are based on those visits.

16. In Trinidad and Tobago and Barbados there are market development grants and export incentive grants respectively that are available to exporters. These grants assist exporters in meeting the cost of overseas promotion and product testing. In Trinidad and Tobago the government provides a 50% level of grant financing for approved projects and it is not subject to corporation taxes.

# APPENDIX 3.A.1
# A TYPICAL EXPORT INCENTIVE SYSTEM

| Export Incentives | Laws and Regulations | Administering Agencies |
|---|---|---|
| 1. Realistic Exchange Rates | · Foreign Exchange Laws | · Ministry of Finance<br>· Central Bank |
| 2. Free Trade Regime for Exporters | · International Trade Law<br>· Tariff Law<br>· Duty Drawback Law<br>· Free Trade Zone Law | · Ministry of Trade and Industry<br>· Commercial Banks |
| 3. Automatic Access to Export Financing | · Banking Regulations<br>· EX-IM Bank Law<br>· Export Credit Insurance Law | · Central Bank<br>· Commercial Banks<br>· Development Banks<br>· EX-IM Bank<br>· Export Credit Insurance Agency |
| 4. Competitive Prices of Primary Inputs | · Labor Law | · Ministry of Labor<br>· Wage Council |
| 5. Compensatory Export Incentives | · Tax Laws<br>· Banking Regulations<br>· Export Estate Development Law<br>· Technical Assistance Regulations | · Ministry of Finance<br>· Central Bank<br>· Commercial Banks<br>· Ministry of Trade and Industry<br>· Ministry of Technology |
| 6. Institutional Support | · Export Association Law<br>· Export Inspection Law<br>· Trade Development Decree | · Ministry of Trade and Industry<br>· Export Associations<br>· Export-Inspection Agency<br>· Trade Development Council |

**Source:** Yung Whee Rhee (1985, p. 17).

**APPENDIX 3.A.2**
**PLOTS OF REAL EFFECTIVE EXCHANGE RATES**
**FOR SELECTED CARICOM COUNTRIES**

Figure 3.1
Barbados's Real Effective Exchange Rate (1968–1989)

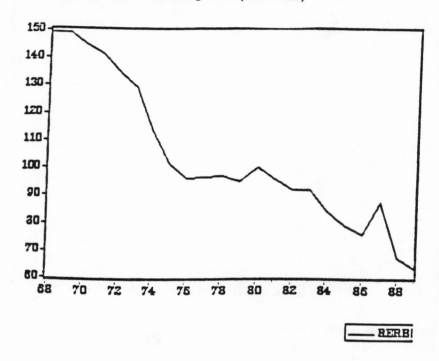

**Figure 3.2**
**Jamaica's Real Effective Exchange Rate (1968–1989)**

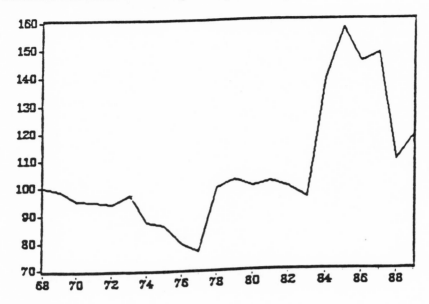

**Figure 3.3**
**Trinidad and Tobago's Real Effective Exchange Rate (1968–1989)**

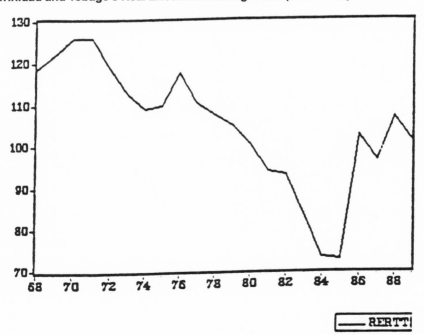

# 4

## Exports and Small Country Growth

A lot of attention has been focused on the relationship between export performance and economic growth in the development economics literature. Generally, two major approaches have been adopted: First, there have been individual country analyses of the implications of export-promotion versus import-substitution strategies for economic growth [see Bhagwati (1978) and Krueger (1978) for useful summaries]. Second, there is a body of empirical research that examines the extent to which differences in export performance may explain intercountry growth differentials—Balassa (1985; 1977), Ram (1985); Feder (1983), Tyler (1981), and Fosu (1990) to mention a few. These studies employ a production function framework that includes exports as an argument in the function. Generally, the empirical evidence suggests that exports have a positive impact on economic growth in developing countries, particularly middle-income and semi-industrialized countries. There have been no studies that focus on small developing countries including the Caribbean countries.

The Caribbean literature on exports and economic growth has generally been cast in the mold of the center periphery model of the "dependency school" that initially evolved in Latin America [Best and Levitt (1968)]. In addition, "staple" theory [see Watkins (1963); Girvan (1972); Beckford (1972)] has been applied in the context of the major mineral exports (i.e., bauxite and oil). Essentially, these studies analyze the developmental impact of foreign-owned (MNC) enclave industries on the domestic economy in Caribbean countries. However, there is no empirical tradition (as mentioned above) for analyzing the relationship between exports and growth. Therefore, given the absence of research on small developing countries in general, and the Caribbean in particular, it is useful to examine empirically the relationship between exports and growth for a cross section of small developing countries including the Caribbean. In Section 4.1 I present Feder's model of exports and growth and apply it to small developing countries. In Section 4.1a data and results are presented for Feder's model. In Section 4.2 an alternative model analyzing the role of exports in output expansion in Caribbean countries is presented. In contrast to Feder's model the importance of the foreign exchange earnings generated by exports is highlighted.

## 4.1 FEDER'S MODEL APPLIED TO SMALL DEVELOPING COUNTRIES

Some empirical studies across countries have shown that developing countries with a strong export growth record have higher rates of economic growth. Tyler (1981) and others have shown that export performance together with other variables are associated with intercountry variance in growth rates. Why is this so? What is special about exports? A variety of explanations have been advanced relating to the beneficial aspects of exports, such as their contribution to greater capacity utilization, technological improvements, better management due to international competition, economies of scale and others. Feder (1983) argues that a major implication of these discussions is that there are substantial differences between marginal factor productivities in export-oriented and non-export-oriented activities, such that the former have higher levels of factor productivity. There are two key propositions to be derived from Feder's model: first, differential marginal factor productivities between the export and nonexport sector; second, dynamic growth effects, that is, "externalities" from the export sector.

An important issue is whether the correlation between export growth and GDP growth is primarily due to joint causation (e.g., you find a new exportable resource, so both exports and GDP rise) or from GDP growth to export growth. Feder's model treats exports as an exogenous variable and is criticized for not considering the issue of simultaneity bias. There is a body of literature on export supply functions that treats exports as an endogenous variable. Therefore, it is argued that exports are a stochastic regressor, and to avoid biased and inconsistent estimates, instrumental variables (two stage least squares, or TSLS) should be employed as the preferred estimating technique. Adams, Behrman, and Boldin (1989) recognize the issue of simultaneity bias and present both TSLS and OLS (ordinary least square) estimates. In the present analysis data for the 1965–1980 period were used as instruments in estimating the model via TSLS for the 1980–1989 period.[1]

Feder's model is an improvement on earlier analyses in that it tries to get at the question of externalities. By so doing it formalizes a lot of anecdotal arguments that have been advanced in support of exports. The model suffers from severe measurement problems since the labor force data are very imprecise and since I/Y (the investment share of GDP) has had to be used as a proxy for the preferred /K. Notwithstanding these problems the model is used here because it provides some analysis of why exports are correlated with growth.

Feder's model develops an analytical framework in which it is possible to quantitatively assess factor productivity differentials between exports and non-exports using aggregate data. Following the empirical approach of the sources of growth studies, aggregate growth is related to changes in labor and capital via an underlying production function. Export performance is also used as one of the variables explaining growth.

A disequilibrium model is developed in which the economy is divided into the export and nonexport sectors. Output in each sector is dependent on factors allocated to that sector, but the nonexport sector is also dependent on the volume of exports produced. This formulation points out the positive effects of exports on other sectors and these effects are regarded as *externalities*.

Because of data limitations in developing countries, sectoral allocations of primary factors are not available, so Feder specified a relationship that permitted estimates of marginal productivities in different sectors using national data (see Appendix 4.A.1 for a full derivation of the model). For econometric purposes Feder estimated the following equation for a sample of countries defined as semi-industrialized.

Where:

$$\dot{Y}/Y = a_0 + \alpha \cdot I/Y + \beta(\dot{L}/L) + \lambda[(\dot{X}/X)\cdot(X/Y)]$$

$$\alpha > 0; \qquad \beta > 0; \qquad \lambda > 0 \tag{1}$$

| Y | = | Output (GDP), |
|---|---|---|
| I | = | Investment, |
| L | = | Labor Force, |
| X | = | Export, and |
| . | = | rate of growth |

Generally, the results provide strong support for the differential marginal factor productivities hypothesis. However, equation (1) does not allow us to identify the specific intersectoral externality effect. For this purpose Feder reformulates the model and estimates the following equation:

$$\dot{Y}/Y = \alpha \cdot I/Y + \beta(\dot{L}/L) + \lambda_1 [\dot{X}/X \cdot X/Y] + \lambda_2 \dot{X}/X$$

$$\alpha > 0; \qquad \beta > 0; \qquad \lambda_1 > 0; \quad \lambda_2 > 0. \tag{2}$$

Where: $\dot{X}/X$ = Export growth rate

## 4.1a  Data and Results

Data for output growth, labor force growth, and export growth, as well as the investment share of GDP, are taken from the *World Development Report* (1991). The World Bank's data for 1965 and 1989 have simply been averaged to obtain a figure for the period 1965–1989, and similarly, have been averaged for 1965 and 1980, as well as 1980 and 1989, to obtain a figure for 1965–1980 and 1980–1989, respectively. For countries in the sample with data available for the whole period, average investment ratios are computed for the periods 1965–1980, 1980–1989, and 1965–1989. These ratios allow some sensitivity analysis to be accomplished. The results do not differ significantly as a consequence of these exercises. Export shares of GDP were also obtained from the *World Development Report* (1991). The periodization used in the empirical work is conditioned by the ready availability of data. Therefore, the model is estimated for the periods 1965–1989, 1965–1980, and 1980–1989 with data available from the *World Development Report* (1991). In addition, the model was developed to analyze growth rates over a period of time as opposed to an annual growth rate, that is, time series data.

An obvious question is how was the sample of small countries chosen, that is, what was the decision rule for inclusion as "small"? Jalan (1982) develops a country size index that allows him to classify fifty-nine countries as an illustrative list of small countries. Generally, this sample is used, but it includes only those countries with populations less than 7 million by 1986 for which data are available. In addition, Israel, Singapore, and Hong Kong are excluded from the sample as their level of development and, in particular, industrial development sets them apart from other small developing countries.

Econometric results are presented for a crosssection of twenty-two small developing countries (see the list of countries and the data set in Appendix 4.A.2) for the time period 1965–1989, twenty-five small developing countries for the subperiod 1965–1980, and twenty-four small developing countries for the ssubperiod1980–1989. The equation is also estimated for fourteen and sixteen small middle-income[2] developing countries drawn from the list of twenty-two, twenty-five, and twenty-four small developing countries for the time periods 1965–1989, 1965–1980, and 1980–1986, respectively. The estimation technique is OLS. A test for heteroscedasticity and the results are presented in Appendix 4.A.3.

Table 4.1 contains the regression results for the chosen small developing countries for the three time periods 1965–1989, 1965–1980, and 1980–1989. The export variables do not perform particularly well and the "externality" variable ($X/X$) is not statistically significant at 10% or better.[3] The change in the export share of GDP is statistically significant in the 1965–1989 period and the 1965–1980 subperiod. The labour force growth variable performs poorly and is not significant in any of the periods. The investment share of GDP is significant in the 1965–1989 period and the 1980–1989 subperiod. A dummy variable is included for CARICOM countries and it is statistically significant. In short, Feder's "externality" argument is not empirically supported in the present sample of small developing countries. The evidence does suggest that in the sample CARICOM countries are different from the other small developing countries.

The results in Table 4.2 are for the periods 1965–1989, 1965–1980, and 1980–1989, but only for a cross section of fourteen, sixteen, and twenty-four small middle-income developing countries, respectively.[4] The results for the small middle-income developing countries are not significantly better than those for the full sample of small developing countries, except for the 1980–1989 subperiod. Once again the performance of the export variables is not good and only the change in the export share of GDP is statistically significant in 1965–1989 and 1980–1989. The performance of the labour force growth variable and the investment share of GDP is weak. The dummy variable for CARICOM countries is not statistically significant, suggesting that it was only significant in the full sample since CARICOM countries are middle-income countries. The equation for the full sample was reestimated with a dummy for middle-income countries, and it was statistically significant at 10% or better.

The test (Park-Glejer) for heteroscedasticity does not detect its presence when the Feder model is estimated for the full sample or the sample of small developing countries in the period under consideration. An important consideration is whether the model applies to different subperiods, since there is no structural break across the two subperiods, 1965–1980 and 1980–1989. To examine this issue the "Chow Test" [Chow (1960)], involving the equality of coefficients of different regressions, is carried out.

The test statistic is the following:

$$\frac{(RSS_R - RSS_{\mu R})/\kappa}{RSS_{\mu R}/(N + M - 2\kappa)}.$$

Where:

N  =  No. of observations in period 1

M  =  No. of observations in period 2

## Table 4.1
## Regression Results for Feder Model Applied to Twenty-Two Small Developing Countries
### [Dependent Variable: Output (GDP) Growth (t-Statistics in parentheses)]

| Right-Hand-Side Variables | 1965–1989 (n = 22) | 1965–1980 (n = 25) | 1980–1989 (n = 24) |
|---|---|---|---|
| INTERCEPT | 0.28 (0.16) | 5.12 (3.95) *** | 0.43 (0.22) |
| I/Y | 0.19 (2.47) ** | -0.03 (-0.42) | 0.14 (1.68) ** |
| L/L | 0.02 (0.03) | 0.15 (0.40) | -0.44 (-0.92) |
| [X/X.X/Y] | 0.04 (1.40) * | 0.13 (2.65) *** | 0.03 (1.00) |
| X/X | -0.14 (-1.01) | -0.16 (-1.77) | 0.09 (0.85) |
| $D^1$ | -4.36 (-3.26) *** | -1.71 (-1.06) | -5.19 (-3.15) *** |
| $R^2$ | 0.57 | 0.31 | 0.63 |
| $R^2$ | 0.44 | 0.13 | 0.53 |

**Notes:** [1]A dummy variable is introduced for CARICOM countries. All tests are one-tailed tests (except for the dummy variable—this means that coefficients with the wrong sign are not statistically significant). ***Means significant at 1% confidence level; **Means significant at 5% confidence level; *Means significant at 10% confidence level.

## Table 4.2
## Regression Results for Feder Model Applied to Small Middle-Income Developing Countries
[Dependent Variable: Output (GDP) Growth (t-Statistics in parentheses)]

| Right-Hand-Side Variables | 1965–1989 (n = 14) | 1965–1980 (n = 16) | 1980–1989 (n = 24) |
|---|---|---|---|
| INTERCEPT | 6.98 (2.40) ** | 8.37 (3.34) *** | 1.59 (1.65) ** |
| I/Y | -0.21 (-2.12) | -0.12 (-1.16) | -0.17 (-1.86) |
| L/L | -0.16 (-0.25) | -0.66 (-1.12) | 0.83 (1.74) ** |
| [X/X.X/Y] | 0.11 (2.78) *** | 0.02 (0.27) | 0.16 (2.96) *** |
| X/X | -0.01 (-0.06) | 0.06 (0.40) | 0.09 (0.86) |
| D | 0.81 (0.71) | 0.48 (0.27) | 1.18 (0.65) |
| $R^2$ | 0.67 | 0.22 | 0.92 |
| $R^2$ | 0.46 | -0.17 | 0.88 |

**Notes:** All t-tests are one-tailed tests (except for the coefficient on the dummy variable); ***Means significant at 1% confidence level; **Means significant at 5% confidence level; *Means significant at 10% confidence level.

$RSS_R$        =        Residual sum of squares (restricted)

$RSS_{\mu R}$        =        Residual sum of squares (unrestricted)

$\kappa$        =        No. of restrictions

The value of the F-statistic is 6.59, which is greater than the critical value of the F-distribution at the 5% level, for which we reject the null hypothesis. Therefore it is incorrect to assume equal coefficients.

In summary, the Feder model performs best in the 1980–1989 period for both samples of countries, based on the explanatory power of the regression, that is, the $R^2$. For the sample of small developing countries, only the change in the export share of GDP variable is significant and this is also true only for the sample of small middle-income developing countries. The important difference is that in the 1980–1989 subperiod for the small middle-income developing countries, the $R^2$ is significantly higher than in any other instance.

The results do not provide strong evidence about the importance of differential marginal factor productivities and "externality" effects in small developing countries. In fact, there is no evidence of the importance of "externalities" of the export sector on the rest of the economy in small developing countries.

As argued earlier, the Feder model highlights the fact that there may be differential marginal factor productivities between the export and the nonexport sector, the marginal factor productivity assumed higher in the export sector. In addition, it points to the potential importance of "externalities" from the export sector to the rest of the economy.

The above analysis does not explicitly recognize the function of exports in developing countries as providing the main source of foreign exchange for the much needed imports of intermediate and capital goods.[5] It is important to note that while the Feder model does not try to identify the extent to which export performance matters (because imports do matter), the fact that imports matter will still show up in Feder's results, mixed in with other reasons why exports may matter. The earlier "two-gap" model literature did recognize the importance of foreign exchange earnings, but suggested that the foreign exchange contribution of exports is important only if the economy suffers from an import "shortage." At present, in many developing countries import rationing is widely used as part of economic policy. In this context a large part of the contribution of exports to GDP growth is due to their role in increasing the supply of foreign exchange and, thus, of imports [see Esfahani (1991)].

## 4.2 OUTPUT AND FOREIGN EXCHANGE FLOWS

Small developing countries are heavily dependent on a wide range of imports of goods and services. In the productive sectors output is heavily dependent on the imports of intermediate and capital goods. Therefore, output expansion necessitates increased quantities of imported intermediate and capital goods and this necessitates increased foreign exchange inflows. In short, a necessary condition for output expansion, both in the short and long-term, is increased foreign exchange flows. Data in Table 2.1 suggest that import shortages may be a constraint to short-term output expansion in CARICOM economies. Note, however, that the argument based on the foreign exchange contribution of exports does not depend on the presence of short-term import shortages. Exports make a vital longer-term contribution to output expansion by providing a supply of foreign exchange to enhance import capacity. This is in contrast to the longer-term reallocative and externality effects highlighted by Feder. A simple production function is hypothesized in which imports (including consumer goods) enter as an argument together with the primary factors, labour and capital. The unavailability of data for the period 1968–1988 does not make it possible to use only intermediate and capital goods imports in the production function analysis. Even the data on total import volume are questionable and, more importantly, the data do not include imported services, which are important if imports are to be included in a production function. Import volume is posited to be a simple function of the real availability of foreign exchange (RF), and in equation (4) below the real foreign exchange variable enters the production function as an argument. The Cobb-Douglas functional form is not initially assumed to be appropriate to CARICOM economies. A more flexible functional form—the Transcendental Logarithmic Production Function (translog) [Christensen, Jorgenson, and Lau (1973)]—is used to test whether the parametric restrictions of a Cobb-Douglas form are valid for CARICOM economies. The results indicate that a Cobb-Douglas form can be used for CARICOM economies. The following model is presented:

$$Y = AK^{\alpha_1} L^{\alpha_2} M^{\alpha_3} \theta^\in \quad \text{(Cobb-Douglas)} \tag{1}$$

$$M = BRF^{\beta_1} B^\mu. \tag{2}$$

Where:

| | | |
|---|---|---|
| Y | = | Real output (GDP) |
| K | = | Capital stock |
| L | = | Labor force |
| M | = | Real imports |
| RF | = | Real gross foreign exchange inflows |

Import capacity is measured as a country's annual real foreign exchange inflows, that is the sum total of all the foreign exchange into a country in a given year. The variable is defined as the country's gross nominal foreign exchange inflows (F) (the sum of gross exports of goods and services plus gross exogenous capital flows) deflated by the country's import price index (PM) to arrive at RF. The *World Tables* [World Bank (1990a)] defines the capacity to import as the value of exports of goods and nonfactor services deflated by the import price index, omitting long-term capital inflows that differentiates it from the above measure. It could also be suggested that one needs to deduct inevitable or compulsory payments on the foreign debt from RF, but, in our case, the data are not available for the period 1968–1988.

Substituting (2) into (1):

$$Y = AK^{\alpha_1}L^{\alpha_2}(BRF^{\beta_1})^{\alpha_3}\theta^{\in} + \mu. \tag{3}$$

Alternative,

$$Y = AB^{\alpha_3}K^{\alpha_1}L^{\alpha_2}RF^{\beta_1^{\alpha_3}}\theta^{\in} + \mu. \tag{4}$$

Therefore,

$$lnY = ln(AB) + \alpha_1 lnK + \alpha_2 lnL + (\alpha_3\beta_1)\, lnRF + v$$

$$\alpha_1 > 0; \quad \alpha_2 > 0; \quad (\alpha_3\beta_1) > 0,\, where\ v = \in + \mu. \tag{5}$$

Initially, the production function analysis is done to test whether the restriction of homogeneity is valid and therefore, whether a Cobb-Douglas structure is appropriate to CARICOM economies.

In the case of the translog there exist cost and production functions that are dual to each other. The aggregate production technology can be empirically investigated using either a production or a cost function. Generally, it is suggested that the cost function be used to estimate the production parameters as it is easier to implement [Binswanger (1974)]. In Appendix 4.A.4 a translog cost function is presented and share equations are derived. A likelihood ratio (LR) test of the restricted versus unrestricted model is done to test whether the parametric restrictions on the share equations are valid. The estimation is done using Barbadian data for the period 1968–1988, and the results of the LR test do not reject the null hypothesis of the restricted model. Therefore, a Cobb-Douglas functional form is appropriate for production technology in Barbados and the same is assumed for Jamaica and Trinidad and Tobago[6] (see Appendix 4.A.4 for the detailed work).

## 4.2a  Data and Results

The data used in the estimation of the model are annual and are obtained from local and international sources. The components of the F-variable are obtained from the IMF's *Balance of Payments Statistics* (1970, 1974, 1979, 1984, 1987, and 1991). The import price index and the domestic price index are obtained from the World Bank's *World Tables* (1989–1990 edition) and the IMF's *International Financial Statistics*, respectively. The labor force data were obtained from the statistics departments in the individual countries and differs from the data used in the Feder analysis. The capital stock data were derived from investment flows and are similar to those used in the Feder analysis. The quality of the labor force data, particularly for the 1970s, is questionable based on discussions I held with officials at the various statistics departments.

Equation (5) is estimated for a pooled cross section time series—Barbados, Jamaica, and Trinidad and Tobago for the period 1968–1988. The periodization is conditioned by the availability of labor force data for the individual countries. In Table 4.3 the OLS results are presented for the pooled sample, and in Table 4.4 the individual country results are presented. To be able to obtain a Durbin-Watson (D.W.) statistic for the pooled regression, sample breaks were created in the data, for example, Jamaica (2–21), Barbados (23–42), Trinidad and Tobago (44–63).

In Table 4.3 the D.W. statistic is 0.36, indicating the presence of serial correlation. Serial correlation is corrected for and the D.W. statistic is now 1.07, the $\bar{R}^2$ is high at 98% but two of the variables—labor and capital—have the wrong sign. The quality of the labor force data is questionable and one must always interpret the results cautiously. The capital stock is derived from investment flows, therefore, the crude nature of the variable might be affecting its performance. In short, the primary factors—labor and capital—have measurement problems that are affecting their performance. The foreign exchange variable is significant at 10% or better with the correct sign. This implies that foreign exchange flows do have a positive impact on domestic output. Foreign exchange flows act as a supply constraint since shortfalls will lower output or reduce supply.

An F-test was done to test the null hypothesis of the restricted model against the alternative of the unrestricted model, but with an F-value of 3.38 we reject the null hypothesis of the restricted model. This is not surprising since the t-statistics on the country intercept dummies are all significant at 1%.

The individual country results in Table 4.4 indicate that the foreign exchange variable is significant in all three countries. The primary factors have the wrong sign in Jamaica and Barbados. They have the correct sign in Trinidad and Tobago but only capital is statistically significant. The $R^2$ ranges from 0.58 in Trinidad and Tobago to 0.96 in Jamaica, which indicates a good performance for the Model. In short, the individual country results support the argument that foreign exchange flows have a positive impact on output over time.

## Table 4.3
## Pooled Regression Results[1] for Some CARICOM Countries
### [Dependent Variable: Log Real GDP (t-Statistics in parentheses)]

| Equation | Constant | LnK | lnI | ln RF | D1 | D2 | $R^2$ | $R^2$ | n | D.W. | F-Statistic |
|---|---|---|---|---|---|---|---|---|---|---|---|
| (1) | 20.87 (7.49) *** | -0.19 (-0.82) | -3.32 (-4.55) | 0.41 (2.75) *** | 8.65 (6.0) *** | 6.73 (7.92) *** | 0.90 | 0.85 | 60 | 0.36 | 66.46 |
| (2) | 3.03 (3.15) ** | 0.10 (1.56) * | 0.88 (-2.66) ** | 0.17 (1.57) * | 1.33 (1.47) ** | 0.69 (1.46) * | 0.99 | 0.98 | 57 | 1.07 | 572.12 |

**Notes:** (All t-tests are one-tailed tests); [1]Barbados is used as the base country so that the country-specific intercepts are deviations from Barbados' intercept; ***Means significant at 1% confidence level; **Means significant at 5% confidence level; *Means significant at 10% confidence level.

## Table 4.4
## Individual Country Results for Some CARICOM Countries (1968–1988)
### [Dependent Variable: Log Real GDP (t-Statistics in parentheses)]

| Equation | Constant | LnK | InI | ln RGFA | $R^2$ | $\bar{R}^2$ | D.W. | Rho[1] | F-Statistic | n |
|---|---|---|---|---|---|---|---|---|---|---|
| (1) Barbados | 7.06 (5.03) *** | -0.08 (-0.89) | -0.25 (-0.84) | 0.20 (4.03) *** | 0.95 | 0.93 | 1.64 | 0.48 (2.32) ** | 63.44 | 20 |
| (2) Jamaica | 35.34 (3.31) *** | -3.55 (-2.38) | -0.87 (-3.26) | 0.41 (1.33) * | 0.96 | 0.94 | 1.48 | 0.61 (3.36) *** | 77.94 | 20 |
| (3) Trinidad and Tobago | 0.14 (0.02) | 0.39 (2.90) *** | 0.13 (0.15) | 0.58 (3.78) *** | 0.58 | 0.50 | 1.18 |  | 7.45 | 21 |

**Notes:** All t-tests are one-tailed tests; [1]Rho is the AR(1) coefficient. Serial correlation is corrected for via the Cochrane-Orcutt procedure. ***Means significant at 1% confidence level; **Means significant at 5% confidence level; *Means significant at 10% confidence level.

Generally, the model of output and foreign exchange flows performs better than the Feder model. There are important differences between the two models that must be noted. Feder's model attempts to analyze growth over a long period across countries, whereas, the model of output and foreign exchange flows is a time series model that analyzes annual changes in output. Thus the Feder-type analysis, where each observation refers to a fairly long period, allows one to pick up the positive effects of high investment rates, whose effects may come with something of a lag. In the analysis using annual data these effects are not likely to show up.

In conclusion the model does provide an alternative explanation about the role of exports in Caribbean-type economies to the Feder model, which stresses the importance of reallocation and "externalities." There is evidence to suggest that in Caribbean economies foreign exchange flows do have a significant influence on domestic output. In this context any source of foreign exchange inflow (including exports) by enhancing import capacity is stimulating economic growth and development. This would seem to be the most important contribution of exports in Caribbean economies.

## NOTES

1. The results are not good and are not presented in the main text. The $R^2$ and adjusted $R^2$ is negative and none of the independent variables are statistically significant at 10% or better.

2. Middle-income economies are those with a GNP per capita of more than US$580 but less than US$6,000 in 1989. Feder (1983) suggests that the correlation between exports and growth is strongest for semi-industrialized economies. Empirical evidence [Adams, Behrman & Boldin (1989)] has found that the Feder model performs better for middle-income developing countries.

3. The weak performance of the export growth variable is consistent with the results of a recent study on exports and growth in Latin America and the Caribbean [Park (1991)]. Park finds no correlation between exports and growth in Latin American and Caribbean countries in the periods 1960–1970 and 1970–1981.

4. The results are presented in Table 4.5 for the low-income countries despite the small number of degrees of freedom.

5. Esfahani (1991) recognizes this as one of the key weaknesses of previous studies looking at the correlation between exports and growth in LDCs. Esfahani argues that the correlation between exports and growth is due mainly to the contribution of exports to the reduction of import "shortages," which restrict the growth of output in many semi-industrialized countries.

6. The absence of data prevented estimation of a translog function for Jamaica and Trinidad and Tobago.

## APPENDIX 4.A.1
## DERIVATION OF FEDER'S MODEL

Following Feder (1983) there are two sectors—exports (X) and nonexports (N). For each sector there is a production function that indicates that output depends on the labor ($L_x$ or $L_n$) and the capital stock used in that sector ($K_x$ or $K_n$). In addition, exports are assumed to have externalities that positively increase nonexport output so:

$$N = F(K_n, L_n, X) \tag{1}$$

$$X + G(K_x, L_x) . \tag{2}$$

Suppose that the ratio of respective marginal factor productivities in the two sectors deviates from unity by a factor of d:

$$(G_K/F_K) = (G_L/F_L) = 1 + \delta, \tag{3}$$

where the subscripts denote partial derivatives.

In the absence of externalities and for a given set of prices if $\delta = 0$, then national output is maximized since marginal factor productivities are equalized across sectors. But there are reasons why one might expect that marginal factor productivities are lower in the nonexport sector (i.e., $\delta > 0$), that is, the more competitive environment in which export firms operate. Note that productivity differentials that are due to externalities are not included in d and they will be clearly identified later on.

Now, differentiating equations (1) and (2):

$$\dot{N} + F_K \cdot I_n + F_L \cdot \dot{L}_n + F_x \cdot \dot{X} \tag{4}$$

$$\dot{X} = G_K \cdot I_x + G_L \cdot \dot{L}_x , \tag{5}$$

where $I_n$ and $I_x$ are sectoral gross investment; and $\dot{L}_n$ and $\dot{L}_x$ are sectoral changes in labor force.

If we denote gross domestic product by Y and given that by definition $Y = N + X$, then

$$\dot{Y} = \dot{N} + \dot{X}. \tag{6}$$

Using equation (3) through (5) in (6) we have:

$$\dot{Y} = F_{KK} \cdot I_n + F_L \cdot \dot{L}_n + F_x \cdot \dot{X} = (1 + \delta) \cdot F_K \cdot I_x + (1 + \delta) \cdot F_L \cdot \dot{L}_x$$

$$= F_K \cdot (I_n + I_x) + F_L \cdot (\dot{L}_n + \dot{L}_x) + F_x \cdot \dot{X} + \delta \cdot (F_K I_x + F_L \cdot \dot{L}_x) . \tag{7}$$

If we define total investment $I(\equiv I_n + I_x)$ and total labor force growth $\dot{L}(\equiv \dot{L}_n + \dot{L}_x)$. Recall that equatio's (3) and (5) imply:

$$F_K \cdot I_x + F_L \cdot \dot{L}_x + \frac{1}{1 + \delta} \cdot (G_K \cdot I_x + G_L \cdot \dot{L}_x) + \frac{\dot{X}}{1 + \delta} . \tag{8}$$

Using this result in equation (7) yields:

$$\dot{Y} + F_K \cdot I + F_L \cdot \dot{L} + (\delta/1 + \delta + F_x) \cdot \dot{X}. \tag{9}$$

Feder (1983) assumes that the marginal product of labor in the nonexport sector is proportional to the average product of labor in the whole economy.

$$F_L = \beta \cdot (Y/L). \tag{10}$$

Then, dividing equation (9) through by $Y$ and denoting $F_K \equiv \alpha$ yields after some manipulation.

$$\dot{Y}/Y = \alpha \cdot (I/Y) + \beta \cdot (\dot{L}/L) + [\delta/(1 + \delta) + F_x] \cdot (\dot{X}/X) \cdot (X/Y) . \tag{11}$$

The coefficient $\alpha$ is to be interpreted as the marginal productivity of capital in the nonexport sector and should therefore be positive but lower than for the economy as a whole [Feder (1983)]. In the absence of "surplus" labor $\beta$ should also have a positive sign. Furthermore, if export activity is really more productive on the margin than other activities, the sign on $(\delta / (1 + \delta) + F_x)$ should also be positive.

One can decompose the factor productivity differential d into its components as follows: The specific intersectoral externality can be identified if we posit a possible specification for $F_x$. If one assumes that exports affect the production of nonexports with constant elasticity.

$$N = F(K_n, L_n, X) = X^\theta , \tag{12}$$

where $\theta$ is a parameter one can show that Equation (11) can now be rewritten:

$$\partial n/\partial x = F_x = \theta \cdot (N/X) \tag{13}$$

$$\dot{Y}/Y = \alpha \cdot \frac{I}{Y} = \beta \frac{i}{L} + \frac{\delta}{1+\delta} + \theta \frac{N}{X} \cdot \frac{\dot{X}}{X} \cdot \frac{X}{Y} \tag{14}$$

but,

$$\theta \cdot \frac{N}{X} = \theta \cdot \frac{N/Y}{X/Y} = \theta \cdot \frac{[1 - (X/Y)]}{(X/Y)} = \frac{\theta}{(X/Y)} - \theta \ . \tag{15}$$

Using this result, equation (14) is rearranged, obtaining

$$\frac{\dot{Y}}{Y} = \alpha \cdot \frac{I}{Y} + \beta \cdot \frac{\dot{L}}{L} + \left( \frac{\delta}{1+\delta} - \theta \right) \frac{\dot{X}}{X} \cdot \frac{X}{Y} + \theta \cdot \frac{\dot{X}}{X} \ . \tag{16}$$

Note that if it is assumed $\delta / (1 + \delta) = \theta$, then the model reduces to

$$\frac{\dot{Y}}{Y} = \alpha \cdot \frac{I}{Y} + \beta \frac{\dot{L}}{L} + \theta - \frac{\dot{X}}{X} \ , \tag{17}$$

which is essentially the model developed by Balassa (1977) and Tyler (1981).

# APPENDIX 4.A.2
# THE LIST OF SMALL COUNTRIES AND THE DATASET
# (1965–1989, 1965–1980, 1980–1989)

**1965–1989**

| Country | Y/Y | L/L | [X/X.X/Y] | I/Y (percent) | X/X |
|---|---|---|---|---|---|
| Bolivia* | 2.3 | 2.6 | 4 | 22 | 1.3 |
| Central American Republic | 2.3 | 2.2 | -8 | 20 | -2.3 |
| Costa Rica* | 4.9 | 2.6 | 12 | 22 | 5.4 |
| Dominican Republic* | 5.8 | 2.5 | 16 | 18 | 0.7 |
| El Salvador* | 2.8 | 2.2 | -14 | 15 | -0.1 |
| Guatemala* | 3.7 | 2.8 | 0 | 13 | -1.8 |
| Haiti | 1.6 | 1.8 | -1 | 10 | 0.6 |
| Honduras* | 3.9 | 3.3 | -5 | 14 | 2.7 |
| Jamaica* | 1.3 | 1.3 | 14 | 28 | -1.1 |
| Kuwait* | 1.2 | 6.1 | -8 | 17 | 11.6 |
| Malawi | 4.4 | 3.1 | 0 | 16 | 4.2 |
| Mali | 4.1 | 2.3 | 4 | 22 | 8.0 |
| Mauritania | 1.8 | 3.9 | 8 | 14 | 3.8 |
| Niger | -0.5 | 2.9 | 8 | 10 | 6.2 |
| Papua New Guinea* | 3.3 | 2.4 | 23 | 22 | 11.0 |
| Paraguay* | 5.1 | 3.0 | 19 | 18 | 6.7 |
| Senegal* | 2.5 | 2.9 | 3 | 13 | 2.6 |
| Sierra Leone | 1.9 | 2.2 | -17 | 11 | -2.4 |
| Mauritius* | 5.0 | 2.4 | 31 | 23 | 6.1 |
| Somalia | 3.3 | 2.8 | -9 | 16 | |
| Trinidad and Tobago* | 0.8 | 1.4 | -18 | 22 | -5.3 |
| Tunisia* | 5.5 | 2.3 | 26 | 25 | 8.1 |

**Note:** Asterisks indicate middle-income countries.

**1965–1980**

| Country | Y/Y | L/L$^1$ | [X/X.X/Y] | I/Y (percent) | X/X |
|---|---|---|---|---|---|
| Bolivia* | 4.4 | 2.5 | -10 | 22 | 2.7 |
| Central American Republic | 2.8 | 1.9 | -9 | 21 | -1.3 |
| Costa Rica* | 6.3 | 2.7 | -2 | 20 | 7.0 |
| Dominican Republic* | 8.0 | 2.7 | -2 | 10 | 0.3 |
| El Salvador* | 4.7 | 2.8 | -4 | 15 | 1.0 |
| Guatemala* | 5.9 | 2.8 | 2 | 13 | 4.8 |
| Haiti | 2.9 | 1.7 | 10 | 7 | 5.5 |
| Honduras* | 5.0 | 3.2 | 5 | 15 | 3.1 |
| Jamaica* | 1.4 | 1.3 | 3 | 27 | -0.4 |
| Kuwait* | 1.6 | 7.1 | 08 | 16 | 18.5 |
| Liberia | 3.3 | 3.0 | 3 | 17 | 4.4 |
| Libya | 4.2 | 4.3 | 10 | 29 | 3.3 |
| Malawi | 5.5 | 2.9 | 4 | 14 | 5.1 |
| Mali | 4.2 | 2.1 | 1 | 18 | 9.5 |
| Mauritania | 2.1 | 2.4 | -14 | 14 | 4.0 |
| Nicaragua* | 2.5 | 3.1 | -4 | 21 | 2.8 |
| Papua New Guinea* | 4.1 | 2.4 | 23 | 22 | 14.1 |
| Paraguay* | 7.0 | 2.8 | -6 | 15 | 6.5 |
| Senegal* | 2.1 | 2.9 | -8 | 12 | 2.6 |
| Sierra Leone | 2.7 | 2.0 | -11 | 12 | -2.4 |
| Mauritius* | 5.2 | 1.6 | 2 | 17 | 3.1 |
| Somalia | 3.5 | 2.6 | 3 | 11 | 4.4 |
| Trinidad and Tobago* | 5.0 | 1.2 | 0 | 21 | -5.5 |
| Tunisia* | 6.5 | 2.1 | 6 | 28 | 10.8 |

**Notes:** Asterisks indicate middle-income countries; $^1$Calculated for 1965–1980.

## Appendix 4.A.2 (Continued)

**1980–1989**

| Country | Y/Y | L/L | [X/X.X/Y] | I/Y (percent) | X/X |
|---|---|---|---|---|---|
| Burkina Faso | 5.0 | 2.6 | -4 | 19 | 0.8 |
| Bolivia* | -0.9 | 2.7 | -6 | 13 | -0.8 |
| Central American Republic | 1.4 | 2.7 | 1 | 9 | -3.7 |
| Costa Rica* | 2.8 | 2.4 | 14 | 24 | 3.1 |
| Dominican Republic* | 2.4 | 2.3 | 18 | 26 | 1.2 |
| El Salvador* | 0.6 | 1.4 | -18 | 16 | -1.6 |
| Guatemala* | 0.4 | 2.9 | -2 | 14 | -11.7 |
| Haiti | -0.5 | 1.9 | -11 | 12 | -6.9 |
| Honduras* | 2.3 | 3.5 | -10 | 13 | 2.1 |
| Jamaica* | 1.2 | 1.3 | 11 | 29 | -2.1 |
| Kuwait* | 0.7 | 4.4 | -4 | 19 | 1.2 |
| Malawi | 2.7 | 3.4 | -4 | 19 | 2.9 |
| Mali | 3.8 | 2.5 | 3 | 27 | 5.6 |
| Mauritania | 1.4 | 2.4 | 22 | 15 | 3.4 |
| Niger | -1.6 | 3.4 | -6 | 10 | -3.8 |
| Papua New Guinea* | 2.1 | 2.5 | 0 | 23 | 6.4 |
| Paraguay* | 2.2 | 3.2 | 25 | 21 | 7.0 |
| Senegal* | 3.1 | 3.0 | 11 | 15 | 2.5 |
| Sierra Leone | 0.6 | 2.4 | -6 | 11 | -2.5 |
| Mauritius* | 5.9 | 1.0 | 29 | 29 | 10.5 |
| Somalia | 3.0 | 3.0 | -12 | 21 | -4.6 |
| Togo | 1.4 | 3.5 | 3 | 21 | 3.1 |
| Trinidad and Tobago* | -5.5 | 1.7 | -18 | 19 | -5.1 |
| Tunisia* | 3.4 | 2.5 | 20 | 23 | 4.1 |

**Sources:** World Bank (1990a) *World Tables* (1989–1990 edition); and World Bank (1991) *World Development Report.*

**Note:** Asterisks indicate middle-income countries.

## APPENDIX 4.A.3
## TEST FOR HETEROSCEDASTICITY

We test for the presence of heteroscedasticity using the Park-Glejer test. Generally,

$$\text{Var } \hat{\epsilon} = E(ee') = \sigma^2 Z^\gamma \tag{1}$$

$$\text{so, } \hat{\epsilon}^2 = \sigma^2 Z^\gamma \tag{2}$$

$$\text{Taking logs: } \ln\hat{\epsilon}^2 = \ln\sigma^2 + \gamma \ln Z \tag{3}$$

$$\Rightarrow \ln\hat{\epsilon}^2 = \alpha + \gamma \ln Z \tag{4}$$

Where $Z$ is the independent variable.

In the Feder model we regress the log of the squared residuals on the log of the I/Y variable. One of the reasons for choosing the I/Y variable is that it has no negative values and we can use logs.

If the I/Y variable is significant at 5% or better, this indicates the presence of heteroscedasticity. If the variable is not significant, we then accept the null hypothesis that the residuals are homoscedastic and there is no heteroscedasticity pesent.

**Table 4.5**

**Regression Results for Feder Model Applied to Small Low-Income Developing Countries**

**[Dependent Variable: Output (GDP) Growth (t-Statistics in Parentheses)]**

| Right-Hand-Side Variables | 1965–1989 (n = 8) | 1965–1980 (n = 9) | 1980–1989 (n = 10) |
|---|---|---|---|
| INTERCEPT | -2.20 (-0.72) | 0.67 (0.27) | 0.97 (0.20) |
| I/Y | 0.20 (1.67) ** | 0.14 1.34 * | 0.19 (1.08) |
| L/L | 0.34 (0.36) | 0.54 (0.55) | -0.82 (-0.68) |
| [X/X.X/Y] | -0.12 (-0.97) | 0.13 (2.26) ** | -0.04 (-0.40) |
| X/X | 0.22 (0.79) | -0.11 (-1.02) | 0.17 (0.50) |
| $R^2$ | 0.64 | 0.65 | 0.58 |
| $R^2$ | 0.17 | 0.30 | 0.25 |

**Table 4.6**

**Park-Glejer Test for Heteroscedasticity[1]**

**[Dependent Variable: Log of Squared Residuals]**

| Right-Hand-Side Variables | Sample of Small Countries | | | Middle-Income Small Countries | | |
|---|---|---|---|---|---|---|
| | 1965–1989 (n = 22) | 1965–1980 (n = 25) | 1980–1989 (n = 24) | 1965–1989 (n = 24) | 1965–1980 (n = 16) | 1980–1989 (n = 14) |
| Intercept | -1.83 (-0.62) | 1.35 (-0.78) | -0.38 (-0.17) | -2.97 (-0.82) | -0.03 (-0.01) | -0.61 (-0.16) |
| LOG I/Y | 0.41 (0.89) | -0.59 (-0.64) | -0.04 (-0.03) | 0.72 (0.57) | -0.04 (-0.03) | -0.01 (-0.01) |
| $R^2$ | 0.01 | 0.02 | 0.00 | 0.01 | 0.00 | 0.00 |

Note: [1]Numbers in parentheses are t-statistics.

## Table 4.7
## Test for Heteroscedasticity[1] for Small Countries
### [Dependent Variable: Squared Residuals]

| Right-Hand-Side Variables | 1965–1989 (n = 22) | | | 1965–1980 (n = 25) | | | 1980–1989 (n = 24) | | |
|---|---|---|---|---|---|---|---|---|---|
| INTERCEPT | -1.34 (-1.11) | -0.94 (-1.94) | -0.98 (-2.36) | -0.11 (-0.07) | -1.76 | -1.84 (-3.12) *** | -0.38 (-0.19) | -0.64 (-1.0) | -0.32 (-0.57) |
| L/L | 0.15 (0.36) | | | -0.50 (-0.98) | | | -0.94 (-1.70) * | | |
| X/X | | 0.01 (0.03) | | | 0.09 (0.74) | | | -0.07 (-0.87) | |
| [X/X.X/Y] | | | 0.01 (0.41) | | | 0.05 (1.41) * | | | 0.08 (1.01) |
| $R^2$ | 0.00 | 0.00 | 0.01 | 0.07 | 0.04 | 0.07 | 0.00 | 0.03 | 0.00 |

Note: [1]t-statistics in parentheses.

**Table 4.8**
**Test for Heteroscedasticity[1] for Small Middle-Income Countries**
**[Dependent Variable: Squared Residuals]**

| Right-Hand-Side Variables | 1965–1989 (n = 14) | | | 1965–1980 (n = 16) | | | 1980–1989 (n = 16) | | |
|---|---|---|---|---|---|---|---|---|---|
| INTERCEPT | -0.11 (-0.07) | -1.84 (-3.12) | -1.76 (-2.57) | -0.09 (0.06) | 0.04 (0.08) | -0.32 (-0.57) | -0.06 (-0.03) | -0.37 (-0.57) | -0.50 (-0.75) |
| L/L | 0.50 (-0.98) | | | -0.16 (-0.29) | | | -0.21 (-0.30) | | |
| X/X | | | 0.09 (0.74) | | | 0.08 (1.01) | | | -0.09 (-0.77) |
| [X/X.X/Y] | | 0.05 (1.41) | | | 0.02 (0.31) | | | -0.04 (-1.07) | |
| $R^2$ | -0.0 | 0.14 | 0.04 | 0.00 | 0.00 | 0.07 | 0.01 | 0.09 | 0.05 |

**Note:** [1]t-statistics in parentheses.

## APPENDIX 4.A.4
## PRODUCTION FUNCTIONS

Generally, the translog cost function has the following form:

$$lnC(w, y) = [a_0 + \sum_{i=1}^{n} a_i lnw_i + \tfrac{1}{2} \sum_{i=1}^{N} \sum_{j=1}^{n} b_{ij} lnw_i lnw_j] + lny$$

$$where: \sum_{i=1}^{n} a_i = 1, \ b_{ij} = b_{ji}, \ \sum_{j=1}^{n} b_{ij} = 0 \quad for \ i = 1,..., n \tag{1}$$

(note: $\underline{w}$ = factor prices; y = output).

If a > 0 for all $i$, $\Sigma a_i = 1$ and $b_{ij} = 0$ for all $i$ and $j$ the translog function collapses to a Cobb-Douglas cost function.

From equation (1) the following factor share equations can be derived.

$$S_{i(w, y)} = a_i + \sum_{j=1}^{n} b_{ij} lnw_j. \tag{2}$$

Of course there is the restriction that:

$$\sum_{j=1}^{n} S_i(w, y) = 1.$$

We can observe $S_i$, so the equation for the factor shares can be used to estimate the parameters of the cost, and hence production, function. If there is homogeneity (Cobb-Douglas form) $b_{ij} = 0$ and equation (2) collapses to:

$$S_{i(w, y)} = a_i. \tag{3}$$

This implies that the factor shares are equal to a constant. In empirical work a time trend variable is added to equation (3) as a simple de-trending procedure. In practice equations (2) and (3) are estimated using a systems estimator (e.g., seemingly unrelated regressions estimator) and a LR test is done to test the validity of the restrictions to determine whether a Cobb-Douglas from is accepted.

We have the following general production function:

$$Q = f(K, L, M),$$ (4)

where:

Q     =     gross output
K     =     capital input
L     =     labor input
M     =     real imports.

It might be suggested that intermediate imports should be included, but reliable data are available only for imports and import prices.

Given the above technology we have the following cost function:

$$lnC = \alpha_0 + lnQ + \alpha_K lnP_K + \alpha lnP_L + \alpha_M lnP_M + \frac{1}{2} \beta_{LL}(lnP_L)^2 +$$

$$\beta_{LK}(lnP_K)(lnP_L) + \beta_{LM}(lnP_L)(lnP_M) + \frac{1}{2}\beta_{MM}(lnP_M)^2 + \beta_{MK}(lnP_K)$$

$$(lnP_M) + \frac{1}{2}\beta_{KK}(lnP_M)^2 .$$ (5)

Differentiating equation (5) with respect to the logs of the prices gives the cost share equations.

$$S_L \equiv \frac{\partial lnC}{\partial lnP_L} = \alpha_L + \beta_{LK}lnP_K + \beta_{LL}lnP_L + \beta_{LM}lnP_M.$$ (6)

$$SK \equiv \frac{\partial lnC}{\partial lnP_K} = \alpha_K + \beta_{KL}lnP_L + \beta_{KK}lnP_K + \beta_{KM}lnP_M.$$ (7)

$$S_M \equiv \frac{\partial lnC}{\partial lnP_M} = \alpha_M + \beta_{LM}lnP_L + \beta_{MK}lnP_K + \beta_{MM}lnP_M.$$ (8)

Since the shares must sum to unity

$$\alpha_K + \alpha_L + \alpha_M = 1$$

and the $\beta$'s sum to zero in each column (row). Therefore, from equation (6) we have:

$$\beta_{LM} = -\beta_{LK} - \beta_{LL}. \tag{9}$$

By substitution in equation (6)

$$S_L = \alpha_L + \beta_{LK}lnP_K - \beta_{LK}lnP_M + \beta_{LL}lnP_L - \beta_{LL}lnP_M. \tag{10}$$

Thus,

$$S_L = \alpha_L + \beta_{LK}(lnP_K - lnP_M) + \beta_{LL}(lnP_L - lnP_M) . \tag{11}$$

$$S_L = \alpha_L + \beta_{LK}(lnP_K/lnP_M) + \beta_{LL}(lnP_L/lnP_M) . \tag{12}$$

Similarly, we can derive:

$$S_K = \alpha_K + \beta_{KK}(lnP_K/lnP_M) + \beta_{KL}(lnP_L/lnP_M) . \tag{13}$$

Therefore, we have a system of two independent equations—equations (12) and (13).

I estimated equations (12) and (13) for Barbados for the period 1968–1988. The purpose here is to test the restriction of homogeneity to determine whether a Cobb-Douglas structure is appropriate.

A critical issue is the estimation technique to be employed. Notwithstanding the fact that OLS estimates will give you unbiased and consistent parameter estimates, it will not be the most efficient. To improve the efficiency of the parameter estimates one should take into account explicitly the correlation of the error terms across equations. Therefore I used Zellner's (1962) seemingly unrelated regressions (SUR) system approach that accounts for possible correlation between equations.

From the results of the SUR estimation we can get the log-likelihood function to carry out the likelihood ratio (LR) test. The LR test uses both the restricted and unrestricted estimators and is based on the following statistic:

$$\lambda_{LR} = 2[L(\hat{\gamma}) - L(\gamma_r)] \xrightarrow{d} \chi_{(j)}^2 ,$$

where:

| | | |
|---|---|---|
| $L(\gamma)$ | = | the unrestricted estimators log-likelihood function |
| $L(\gamma_r)$ | = | the restricted estimators log-likelihood function |

The system of share equations—equations (12) and (13)—are estimated for both the restricted and unrestricted model by SUR. Note that equations (12) and (13) are the unrestricted model. The restricted model that is estimated is the following:

$$S_L = \alpha_L + bt, \tag{14}$$

where t = time trend

$$S_K = \alpha_K + ct. \tag{15}$$

With a test statistic of 4.01 we accept the null hypothesis of the restricted model at a 95% level of confidence ($\xi^2_{0.95} = 8.672$).

# 5

## Determinants of the Caribbean's Export Performance

The descriptive analysis of the CARICOM countries recent export performance (1968–1988) indicates weak performance, particularly in the 1979–1988 sub-period. The export performance deteriorated in the 1980s for total merchandise exports and manufactured exports. The main purpose of this chapter is to isolate some of the major variables influencing the region's export performance. The analysis will highlight the importance of "incentives" to export performance, particularly the exchange rate.

In the trade and development literature a variety of approaches have been adopted in analyzing developing countries' export performance. A common approach is time series (regression) analysis of export supply functions. The model is a single equation export supply function that is based on the "small country" assumption (i.e., small countries are "price takers" in the international market so export demand is infinitely elastic). Among the studies using this methodology for analyzing developing countries export performance are Donges and Riedel (1977), Krueger (1978), Yang (1981), Ali (1979). In the case of the Caribbean countries[1] there is no published research analyzing export performance via export supply functions.[2]

Given the limited research that has been done, there is a need to analyze the Caribbean's export performance more closely. In addition, given the contemporary weak export performance in the region and the arguments for greater export diversification, the results may provide some policy insights into a successful export strategy. This chapter is arranged as follows: Section 5.1 briefly reviews the literature on the microfoundations of the export supply function. This is followed in the Section 5.2 by a discussion of the model specification to be used. In Section 5.3, econometric results are presented for individual (nontraditional) and aggregate export supply equations. Finally, the results are interpreted and some conclusions are drawn.

## 5.1 MODEL OF EXPORT SUPPLY: THEORETICAL DISCUSSION

Goldstein and Khan (1984), in a review of trade models, argue that the standard approach to specifying and estimating foreign trade equations for both developed and developing countries is the "imperfect substitutes" model, in which the key assumption is that neither imports nor exports are perfect substitutes for domestic goods. (See Appendix 5.A.1 for a fuller description of the imperfect substitutes model).

The imperfect substitutes model specifies demand and supply functions arriving at reduced form solutions.[3] On the demand side, the consumer is assumed to maximize utility subject to a budget constraint. The resulting demand function for imports depends on income in the home country, the price of the imported good, and the price of the domestic substitute.

Export supply functions that are estimated are reduced form equations derived from the imperfect substitutes model. In many instances export demand is assumed to be infinitely elastic for developing countries (i.e., developing countries are price-takers on the international market). This is the familiar "small country" assumption. The specification of the export supply function in the imperfect substitutes model [i.e., equations (3) and (4)] is quite straightforward. The producer is assumed to maximize profits subject to a cost constraint. The reduced form equation that is derived posits an export supply function that depends positively on the price of exports, negatively on input prices, and positively on productive capacity.

The central idea behind the supply function in the model is that the supply of exports will increase with the profitability of producing and selling exports. The domestic price index (P) serves a dual role in the supply functions. First, assuming a given export price, the profitability of export industries falls when factor costs in these industries increases. Generally, these factor costs follow the general level of domestic prices so P serves as a proxy for them. This implies that production for export will respond to P. Second, an increase in domestic prices[4] will result in a fall in the relative profitability of selling for export rather than on domestic markets. In the conventional model a relative variable (PX/PD) is used to capture the above idea. The variable PX is an index of effective export prices in local currency, where; PX = PE.ER. That is, the effective export price is an index of prices received by exporters in foreign currency (PE) multiplied by the effective exchange rate (ER). The ER is defined to be the official exchange rate plus all export subsidies—direct export subsidies, tax exemption, preferential export loans, and so forth. The variable PD is an index of domestic wholesale prices.

The short-run effect of domestic demand pressure on export supply has been a controversial issue in the literature. Some argue that domestic demand does not affect exports in the short run. Others argue that domestic demand affects exports via its effect on relative prices. Therefore, an export supply equation that includes a relative price variable should not have an additional variable that measures domestic demand pressure. Another approach argues that domestic demand has a direct effect on exports and not just an indirect influence via a relative price effect. Empirical studies in LDCs and semi-industrialized countries have found some empirical support for the inclusion of a domestic demand pressure variable [See Donges and Riedel (1977); Yang (1981); Zilberfarb (1980)]. Generally, a measure of capacity utilization is used to proxy the effect of domestic demand pressure on export supply. The argument is that increased capacity utilization is indicative of a higher level of domestic demand in the short run, resulting in reduced supply to the export market.

Despite the widespread application of the standard export supply function in the literature, some researchers have tried to rest the model on even firmer or more developed microfoundations. There is a literature—Kohli (1978), Diewert and Morrison (1986), and Faini (1988)—that has helped root export decisions more firmly in well-established microeconomic theory. The models developed by Kohli and Diewert and Morrison estimate the demand for imports and supply of exports simultaneously. The technology is specified with imports as an input and the import demand derived and export supply equations are estimated simultaneously, with the demand equations for labor and capital subject to symmetry and homogeneity. This approach does not include domestic demand pressure as an explanatory variable in the export supply equation.

Faini clarifies the absence of domestic demand pressure in these models as an explanatory variable. From a theoretical choice model of the firm, Faini derives the conditions under which capacity utilization may affect export supply. In the model, the firm chooses, first, the level of productive capacity and then, one period later, determines production and allocation between domestic and foreign markets on the basis of realized prices, demand conditions, and installed capacity. It is assumed that the cost of a man period is a function of the number of hours worked, possibly reflecting the existence of overtime payments when actual hours exceed a given norm ("standard" hours). As a consequence unexpected increases in domestic absorption will lead to higher costs and lower exports.

Many previous studies estimating the export supply function, notably Donges and Riedel (1977), Krueger (1978), and Yang (1981), have employed similar models. Empirical specifications vary in these studies but the basic model is the following:

$$\log X_t = \beta_0 + \beta_1 \log (PX/PD)_t + \beta_2 \log IP_t + \beta_3 \log CU_t = U_t$$

$$\beta_1 > 0; \quad \beta_2 > 0; \quad \beta_3 > 0. \tag{1}$$

Where:

| | | |
|---|---|---|
| X | = | exports (constant price) |
| PX | = | an index of effective export prices in local currency, where; PX = PE.ER |
| PD | = | an index of domestic wholesale prices |
| IP | = | an index of total industrial production (a proxy for the capacity to produce) |
| CU | = | a measure of economy-wide capacity utilization (as a proxy for domestic demand pressure) |
| t | = | time subscripts. |

In summary, the conventional single equation model of export supply is derived as a reduced form equation in the imperfect substitutes model. In many empirical studies the equation is modified to include a domestic demand pressure variable. Recently, some researchers have been concerned that the export supply function has not been derived from a well-defined set of relevant hypotheses on technology and market structure and have developed models rooting export decisions in microeconomic theory. Faini (1988) argues that these models are implicitly based on the assumption of market-clearing prices and leave no role for domestic demand pressure. Faini develops a micromodel of a representative firm and derives the conditions under which capacity utilization may affect export supply. In short, the theoretical literature is being developed to provide stronger micro foundations for the traditional export supply model.

## 5.2 MODEL SPECIFICATION

The model employed in this study makes the small country assumption that the country is assumed to face an infinitely elastic demand for its exports, so that changes in foreign demand can influence exports only through changes in world prices. Thus, the model posits that export volumes are determined by supply-side variables. The diagram at the top of page 111 illustrates the basic model.

On the vertical axis is the relative price of exports in domestic currency. That is, the world price multiplied by the exchange rate deflated by local prices. Changes in world prices or in the exchange rate over time would lead to a new

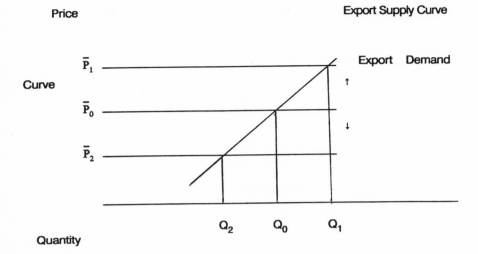

Price                                                    Export Supply Curve

Curve

$\bar{P}_1$

$\bar{P}_0$

$\bar{P}_2$

Export   Demand

$Q_2$      $Q_0$      $Q_1$

Quantity

quantity supplied of exports for the small country (e.g., $Q_0$, $Q_1$, or $Q_2$). In the diagram changes in the world price to $\bar{P}_1$ or $\bar{P}_2$ can result from a change in the world market price or an exchange rate change. An exchange rate devaluation would increase the world price in domestic currency and lead to a price increase from $\bar{P}_0$ to $\bar{P}_1$ and quantity supplied from $Q_0$ to $Q_1$.

In the single equation model of export supply [i.e., equation (1)] the effective export price is an index of prices received by exporters in foreign currency (PE) multiplied by the effective exchange rate (ER). The use of PD, an index of wholesale prices, as a divisor to PX captures the competition from the suppliers standpoint between exports and domestic sales. In short, the relative price PX/PD measures the relative profitability of exports. It is extremely difficult to obtain or develop time series data on export subsidies, and preferential export credits for Caribbean countries.[5] Therefore, the real effective exchange rate (REER) was used in the model. The REER measures the domestic price of a country's tradable goods (import substitutes as well as exports) relative to nontradable goods over time. The REER is calculated as the inflation adjusted weighted average of changes in nominal exchange rates of an individual country's currency, vis-à-vis all other countries that are important export markets of the individual country. Using the arithmetic averaging technique, the following definition of the REER results.

$$REER = 100 \cdot \sum_{i-1}^{n} W_i \cdot (E_{it} E_{io}) \cdot (P_{it}/P_{io}) ,$$

where $W_i$ = the normalized export weight and is defined as:

$$W_i = X_i / \sum_{i-1}^{n} X_i \, ,$$

where $X_i =$ is the export of commodity I and,

$$\sum_{i=1}^{n} W_i = 1.$$

| $(E_{it}/E_{io})$ | = | an index of the price of the $i^{th}$ trading partners currency in terms of the home currency in period $t$ relative to base year 0. |
| $(P_{it}/P_{io})$ | = | the ratio of the price index of the $i^{th}$ trading partner in period $t$ relative to the price index of the home country in period $t$ with the base year 0. |

In this standard formulation of the REER, the critical feature in terms of economic meaning is the weighting procedure employed. Maciejewski argues that "to be economically meaningful the index must capture the type of competitive relationship that predominates in the major international markets in which the reporting country is affectively competing." To try to achieve this objective, three basic weighting procedures are suggested by Maciejewski (1983: 505).

| Competitors | Adequate Weighting Procedures |
|---|---|
| (a) Domestic producers in the importing markets are the main competitors | (a) Trade export weights that reflect the shares of a country's major export markets in total export |
| (b) Other countries selling to the same importing markets are the main competitors | (b) Weights that reflect the shares of other exporters in markets of interest to countries under study |
| (c) Both domestic producers and other exporters to importing markets are the main competitors; in this case all suppliers are relevant | (c) Weights that reflect effectively competing shares of domestic producers and of other exporters in markets of interest to the country under study |

The REER is defined using weighting procedures (a) and (b). The former is applied to both the individual and aggregate export supply equations. The latter is applied specifically to the individual export supply equation.

An increase means a real depreciation (or an increase in the relative price of tradables) that should induce an increase in export supply. Therefore, a positive relationship between exports and the REER is postulated. It is assumed that the REER is a policy variable (exogenous) in the sense that movements in the nominal exchange rate by policymakers can appreciate or depreciate the REER.

Estimates of a country's capital stock are used as a proxy for capacity to produce. The methodology used to derive capital stock estimates (constant value) in a common currency ($US) across the sample of countries is presented in Appendix 5.A.2. A larger productive capacity is assumed to increase output and thus the ability to supply export markets.

Generally, the domestic demand pressure variable has been proxied by a measure of capacity utilization (CU). In some studies [Donges & Riedel (1977)] the CU variable is defined as the deviation from the semilog time trend of industrial production.

In some studies [see Donges and Riedel (1977); Yang (1981)] the industrial production index is used as a proxy for the economy's capacity to produce. Both studies cited the potential for a multicollinearity problem between the CU measure and the proxy for the capacity to produce (i.e., the industrial production index). In fact, Donges and Riedel detect the presence of multicollinearity and do not interpret the coefficient on the domestic demand pressure variable.

The use of the industrial production index is only justifiable as a measure of capacity if exports consist mostly of manufactured products. This is not the case in Caribbean countries; thus, overall GDP is used. The Wharton Index of Capacity Utilization is used as the measure of capacity utilization. The index is defined as follows:

$$CU = \frac{Y}{Y*} \, 100. \tag{2}$$

Where:

$$Y \quad = \quad \text{real GDP}$$
$$Y^* \quad = \quad \text{capacity}$$

$Y^*$ is calculated from the real GDP data for the individual countries. The peak points of the series are identified and the peaks are joined by interpolating between the peak points.

Following the conventional model it is suggested that increased capacity utilization indicates high domestic demand and low export supply, thus, one would expect a negative correlation between exports and capacity utilization.

The estimating equation is as follows:

$$lnX = \beta_0 + \beta_1 \ln REER + \beta_2 \, lnK + \beta_3 \, lnCU$$

$$\beta_1 > 0; \quad \beta_2 > 0; \quad \beta_3 < 0. \tag{3}$$

Where:

REER     =      real effective exchange rate based on trade partners export weights

K      =      aggregate capital stock

CU      =      capacity utilization index

X      =      exports (constant price)

Goldstein and Khan (1984) argue that there is no strong theoretical reason for using the log-linear version of the supply equation, except that the regression fit is usually better. In addition, the parameter estimates are the elasticities. This is useful for the present study since the supply elasticities with respect to the REER are of considerable interest. The issue of dynamic adjustment was considered in specifying the model. It was recognized that exports might respond with a lag to changes in incentives. However, estimation of a partial adjustment model did not result in improved or better results.

## 5.3 NONTRADITIONAL EXPORTS

Generally, the export supply model is applied to manufactured exports [see Donges and Riedel (1977); Ali (1979)] or nontraditional exports [Yang (1981)]. There are different arguments advanced in the literature for the concentration on nontraditional exports. First, in many instances primary exports are guided by commodity agreements, preferential trading arrangements or quotas, so suppliers are constrained by some nonmarket mechanism. This is also true for some manufactured exports—clothing—but this is not as widespread. Second, it is felt that total real exports is far too aggregative. Third, from a policy point of view the emphasis is frequently on the development of nontraditional exports so the emphasis should be on these exports.

In the case of Caribbean countries there are four main types of exports:

     1. Primary exports—mainly bauxite, bananas, and sugar

2. Fuels—primarily petroleum from Trinidad and Tobago

3. Simple light manufactures—mainly clothing, toys, paper products and, to a lesser extent, furniture

4. Services—basically tourism

Types 1, 2, and 4 are traditional exports, and 3 is the major nontraditional export.[6] Nontraditional exports may be considered under the following classifications:

1. Clothing (SITC 84)—mainly "807" exports[7]—from Jamaica, Barbados, Costa Rica, and the Dominican Republic

2. Miscellaneous manufactures (SITC 89)—including toys, paper products, sound recorders—from Jamaica and Barbados

3. Information processing services—mainly data processing—from Jamaica, Dominican Republic, and, to a lesser extent, Barbados

4. Resource-based heavy industry—ammonia, methanol, urea, fertilizers, steel rods—from Trinidad and Tobago.

The information processing industries are of recent vintage, having started exporting in the 1980s, and there are few data on these industries. The resource-based industries are concentrated in Trinidad and Tobago and are unique to that country. The concentration here is therefore on the conventional labor-intensive manufactures for developing countries—clothing (SITC 84) and miscellaneous manufactures (SITC 89).

A similar model to that in equation (3) is used for the estimation of individual industry-specific export equations but with some modifications to the measurement of the REER variable. In particular, consistent with the recommendations on weighting procedures by Maciejewski (1983), the weights are changed to more closely reflect the competitive circumstances of individual exports.

Clothing is one of the most important manufactured exports from the Caribbean countries particularly to the United States.[8] The data in Tables 5.1a and 5.1b point out the importance of the U.S. market to the CARICOM clothing industry. Barbados and Jamaica are the only two significant clothing exporters from the English-speaking Caribbean countries to the United States.

Generally, one can identify three sets of "competitors" facing Caribbean clothing exporters in the U.S. market.

1. Domestic U.S. producers

2. Developed country suppliers

3. Developing country suppliers

| Table 5.1a Exports to the United States as a Percentage of Total Clothing Exports: Jamaica and Barbados | | | |
|---|---|---|---|
| Country | 1970 | 1979 | 1988 |
| Barbados | 42% | 58% | 89% |
| Jamaica | 80% | 52% | 81% |

**Source:** Calculated from U.N. Commodity Trade Statistics.

| Table 5.1b The Share of Textiles and Clothing Exports to the United States as a Percentage of Total Manufactured Exports to the United States: Jamaica and Barbados | | | |
|---|---|---|---|
| Country | Share in Manufacturing Exports | | Annual Growth Rate |
| | 1980 | 1986 | |
| Barbados | 28.0 | 18.5 | 3.3 |
| Jamaica | 68.6 | 71.9 | 38.8 |

**Source:** World Bank (1988) p. 13.

The present analysis does not consider (a) and (b) in the REER weighting procedure. The rationale is that the simple labor intensive products sold by Caribbean exporters are qualitatively differentiated from those sold by exporters belonging to 1 and 2. Another differentiating factor is the greater tolerance for imports from developed country suppliers in the U.S. market. Generally, one finds that developing country suppliers are more subject to protective measures—quotas and voluntary export restraints (VERs).

Given the above arguments the weighting procedure adopted in calculating the industry-specific REERs reflects the export shares of developing country suppliers in the U.S. market. However, the U.S. market is highly regulated and many developing country suppliers are supply-constrained (e.g., through the Multi-Fibre Arrangement). The export weights that are used must reflect the shares of those developing country suppliers that are not supply-constrained. To identify this set of suppliers requires more careful analysis of the U.S. clothing market.

## 5.3a  U.S. Clothing Market

The U.S. clothing market is heavily quota-constrained. The principal obstacle to free trade in this market is the Multi-Fibre Arrangement.[9] Under this arrangement some developing countries are heavily quota-constrained, particularly the major clothing exporters to the United States—Korea, Taiwan, and Hong Kong. Since, there are well-defined limits to the extent that they can expand export volume, that is, they are quota-constrained, these countries are not considered as "competitors" for the Caribbean. Under the MFA a number of other developing countries also have bilateral quotas with the United States. Data provided by the World Bank indicate which developing countries have faced bilateral quotas between 1981 and 1987. The data in Table 5.2 allow one to derive a list of unconstrained clothing exporters to the United States for the years 1981–1987. Countries that did not face quotas for most of the years during the period 1981–1987 were included in the list of unconstrained suppliers. In addition, developing countries not in Table 5.2 or those affected by the MFA, but still exporting to the United States, were also included. These countries were derived by matching Table 5.2 with the list of SITC 84 exporters to the United States for each year between 1981–1987. The list of unconstrained suppliers is presented in Table 5.3.

An important issue to be considered in examining the performance of Caribbean clothing exports in the U.S. market is the relationship between the Caribbean Basin Initiative (CBI) and Tariff item 807. The 807 program has no specific U.S. content requirement and simply relates to the base for the application of the customs tariff. Essentially, the value of U.S. components used in the production of export products is exempt from U.S. customs duties.

The Caribbean Basin Economic Recovery Act, referred to as the CBI, took effect in January 1984. The CBI grants duty-free treatment to U.S. imports from twenty-two Caribbean basin countries for twelve years. To receive duty-free treatment the item must be grown, produced, or manufactured in a beneficiary country and meet "rules-of-origin" requirements:

1. The item must be imported directly from a beneficiary.
2. At least 35% of the value of the item must be added in one or more beneficiary.
3. The product must be substantially transformed in one or more beneficiary. In the case of the 35% value-added requirement, it is permissible for U.S.-made components to comprise 15% of the 35%.

The CBI *does* deny duty-free treatment for a specific list of products. Items exempted from the duty-free treatment are shown in Table 5.4. At the outset, Caribbean countries argued strongly that the exclusion of garments and foot-

**Table 5.2**
**Developing Suppliers Subject to Bilateral Quotas in**
**Textile Products in the United States**

| Country | 1981 | 1982 | 1983 | 1984 | 1985 | 1986 | 1987 |
|---|---|---|---|---|---|---|---|
| Argentina | | | | | | | |
| Bangladesh | | | | | | x | x |
| Barbados | | | | x | | | |
| Brazil | x | x | x | $x^d$ | x | x | x |
| Burma | | | | | | | |
| China | x | x | x | x | x | x | x |
| Colombia | x | x | x | x | $x^d$ | x | x |
| Costa Rica | x | x | x | x | x | x | x |
| Dominican Rep. | x | x | x | x | $x^d$ | x | x |
| Egypt | $x_b$ | $x^b$ | $x^b$ | x | x | x | x |
| El Salvador | | | | | | | x |
| Guam | | | | | $x^a$ | $x^a$ | $x^a$ |
| Guatemala | | | | | x | x | x |
| Haiti | x | x | x | x | x | x | x |
| Hong Kong | x | x | x | x | x | x | x |
| India | x | x | x | x | x | x | x |
| Indonesia | | x | x | x | $x^d$ | x | x |
| Jamaica | | | | | | | x |
| Korea, Rep. of | | | | | | | |
|   Korea, D.P.R. | x | x | x | x | x | x | x |
| Macao | x | x | x | x | x | x | x |
| Malaysia | x | x | x | x | x | x | x |
| Maldive Islands | | $x^d$ | x | $x^d$ | x | $x^d$ | |
| Malta | | | | | | | |
| Mauritius | | $x^b$ | $x^a$ | x | $x^d$ | x | x |
| Mexico | x | x | x | x | x | x | x |
| Nepal | | | | | | x | x |
| Pacific Islands | | | | | $x^a$ | | |
| Pakistan | x | x | x | x | x | x | x |
| Panama | | | | x | x | x | x |
| Peru | | | | x | x | x | x |
| Philippines | x | x | x | x | x | x | x |
| Romania | x | x | x | x | x | x | x |
| Singapore | x | x | x | x | x | x | x |
| Sri Lanka | x | x | x | x | x | x | x |
| Taiwan | x | x | x | x | x | x | x |
| Thailand | x | x | x | x | x | x | x |
| Trinidad & Tobago | | | | | | x | |
| Turkey | | | | | x | x | x |
| Uruguay | | | | x | x | x | x |
| Vietnam | | | | | | | |
| Yugoslavia | x | x | x | x | x | x | x |

**Source:** World Bank Computer Files on the MFA.

**Notes:** X = Years subject to bilateral quota; a = Years subject only to an aggregate quota; b = Subject only to monitoring; no quota limit; c = Restrictions on value (as opposed to volume) of imports; d = Data not available.

**Table 5.3**
**Unconstrained Suppliers of Textiles to the U.S. Market 1968–1988[10]**

| Group 1 (Unconstrained Suppliers) | |
|---|---|
| Argentina | Peru |
| Barbados | Trinidad and Tobago |
| El Salvador | Turkey |
| Guatemala | Uruguay |
| Jamaica | Morocco |
| Malta | Bolivia |
| Mauritius | Honduras |

**Table 5.4**
**Exempted Items from the CBI Duty-free Treatment**

| | Items | Range of U.S. Tariff Rates |
|---|---|---|
| (a) | Textiles and apparel articles which are subject to the MFA. | 5–40% |
| (b) | Footwear, handbags, luggage, flat goods, work gloves, and leather wearing apparel. | 2–40% |
| (c) | Canned tuna. | 6–35% |
| (d) | Petroleum and products derived from petroleum. | 0.3–1.6% |
| (e) | Watches and watch parts that use material originating in a communist country. | 5–20% |

**Source:** World Bank (1988) p. 68.

wear, in particular, from the CBI's duty-free treatment deprived the region of major potential gains for its major nontraditional exports. These complaints by Caribbean countries led to two efforts by the United States to improve the Caribbean's access to its market. First, the U.S. government implemented a special regime for the Caribbean's garment industry, allowing re-export on special terms to the United States of garments assembled from fabric made and cut in the United States. Bilateral treaties were developed between the U.S.

government and Caribbean states and the Caribbean states were given "guaranteed access levels" (GALs) for specified quantities of garments, with duty paid in the United States only on the value added by assembly. Countries that negotiated GALs are also known as operating under "super 807" rules of origin. That is, the 807 provision was amended for Caribbean countries falling under the CBI to permit the availability of these GALs. They are also allowed to ship agreed quantities produced from fabric made in other countries.

Second, in 1989 the U.S. government administration asked Congress to improve the CBI. It proposed the removal of the twelve-year trade limit on the trade program for some textile products and reduced duties on others. It also guaranteed CBI sugar quotas at no less than 1989 levels. But a strong domestic lobby in the United States defeated the proposals for duty relief for garments and textiles.

In summary, it appears that the Caribbean clothing exports to the United States face two trade regimes: the 807 and an additional "special" regime, the GALs.

In Appendix 5.A.3 the plots of clothing exports to the U.S. market for Costa Rica, Jamaica, and the Dominican Republic in the period 1968–1988, show a sharp upward trend in exports, particularly after 1982. Officials at the Export Promotion Organization in Jamaica (JAMPRO) suggest that there was the perception of increased market access for clothing exports among foreign investors after the introduction of the CBI and particularly after the negotiation of the GALs. One then saw new firms, mainly from Hong Kong, locating in Jamaica, particularly at the Export Processing Zone in Kingston. There was no distinct upward trend in clothing exports from Barbados to the United States after 1982. Officials at the Barbados Export Promotion Corporation (BEPC) suggest that they were unable to attract clothing firms to Barbados after the introduction of the CBI as Jamaica, Costa Rica and the Dominican Republic had done. The major reason cited by the officials was the significantly higher U.S. dollar wage costs in Barbados relative to those countries.

### 5.3b Industry-Specific Export Equation: Clothing

The REER is derived using weighing procedures 1 and 2 referred to earlier in this chapter. On the basis of these two measures, REER and REER1 are used in the estimation of equation (8). REER1 reflects the export share of unconstrained developing country suppliers in the U.S. clothing market and group 1 weights are used in the calculation of REER1. Groups 2, 3, and 4 are subsets of the countries in Group 1 based on simple geographical distinctions. Weights based on these groups were also employed on an experimental basis, and the econometric results are footnoted. The REER measure using weighting procedure 1 (defined as REER in the chapter) captures the competition of domestic producers in the importing markets, as opposed to developing country competitors in a single market. Complementary to the above analysis, partial correlation matrices of the REERs using the different weighting schemes are now presented for each country in Table 5.5. The purpose is to examine whether the different weights really create a substantial difference in the REER variable. The results differed across the four countries, but especially for Barbados. Generally, the partial correlation matrices indicate that the weights do significantly distinguish the various REER measures, except in the case of Barbados where the correlation between REER and REER1 is 0.92. One should note that Barbados has always maintained a fixed exchange rate with the U.S. dollar and never devalued its currency. As stated earlier, the key correlation statistic is between REER and REER1 since the weights used in REER2, REER3, and REER4 are subsets of the weights used in REER1. The correlation between REER and REER1 range from 0.52 for Costa Rica to 0.92 for Barbados, with the Dominican Republic and Jamaica being 0.66 and 0.56, respectively.

Given the absence of data on capital stocks in the manufacturing sector of these countries, the estimates of the aggregate capital stock was used. In addition, a capacity utilization measure is used to proxy the effect of domestic demand pressure on exports. The capacity utilization measure is calculated as a Wharton Index of Capacity Utilization using value added in manufacturing. Once again country dummies are introduced for country-specific intercepts.

The estimating equation is the following:

$$lnCX = a_0 + a_1\ lnREER + a_2\ lnK + a_3\ lnCUM + a_4\ D_1 + a_5\ D_2 + a_6\ D_3$$

$$a_1 > 0; \quad a_2 > 0; \quad a_3 < 0. \tag{8}$$

Where:

| | | |
|---|---|---|
| $D_1$ | = | Jamaica's country dummy |
| $D_2$ | = | Dominican Republic's country dummy |
| $D_3$ | = | Costa Rica's country dummy |
| CUM | = | capacity utilization in manufacturing |
| CX | = | clothing exports to the United States (constant price) |
| REER | = | real effective exchange rate (competitor weighted) |
| K | = | capital stock (constant price) |

Barbados is used as the base country. Therefore the intercepts reported are the deviations between Barbados and individual country intercepts.

## Table 5.5
## Partial Correlation Matrix for the Real Effective Exchange Rate
## Using Different Weights: Selected Countries

### (a) Jamaica

|        | REERJ | REER1 | REER2 | REER3 | REER4 |
|--------|-------|-------|-------|-------|-------|
| REERJ  | 1.00  | 0.56  | 0.40  | 0.64  | 0.30  |
| REERJ1 | 0.56  | 1.00  | 0.78  | 0.64  | 0.68  |
| REERJ2 | 0.40  | 0.78  | 1.00  | 0.56  | 0.68  |
| REERJ3 | 0.64  | 0.64  | 0.56  | 1.00  | 0.38  |
| REERJ4 | 0.30  | 0.68  | 0.68  | 0.38  | 1.00  |

### (b) Barbados

|       | REERB | REER1 | REER2 | REER3 | REER4 |
|-------|-------|-------|-------|-------|-------|
| REERB | 1.00  | 0.92  | 0.90  | 0.12  | 0.84  |
| REER1 | 0.92  | 1.00  | 0.97  | 0.18  | 0.95  |
| REER2 | 0.90  | 0.97  | 1.00  | 0.13  | 0.91  |
| REER3 | 0.12  | 0.18  | 0.13  | 1.00  | 0.16  |
| REER4 | 0.84  | 0.95  | 0.91  | 0.16  | 1.00  |

## Table 5.5 (continued)

### (c) Dominican Republic

|  | REERDR | REER1 | REER2 | REER3 | REER4 |
|---|---|---|---|---|---|
| REERDR | 1.00 | 0.66 | 0.25 | 0.51 | 0.45 |
| REERJ1 | 0.66 | 1.00 | 0.51 | 0.95 | 0.10 |
| REERJ2 | 0.25 | 0.51 | 1.00 | 0.53 | -0.31 |
| REERJ3 | 0.51 | 0.95 | 0.53 | 1.00 | 0.01 |
| REERJ4 | 0.45 | 0.10 | -0.31 | 0.01 | 1.00 |

### (d) Costa Rica

|  | REERCR | REER1 | REER2 | REER3 | REER4 |
|---|---|---|---|---|---|
| REERCR | 1.00 | 0.52 | 0.72 | 0.86 | 0.54 |
| REER1 | 0.52 | 1.00 | 0.79 | 0.67 | 0.81 |
| REER2 | 0.72 | 0.79 | 1.00 | 0.70 | 0.89 |
| REER3 | 0.86 | 0.67 | 0.70 | 1.00 | 0.56 |
| REER4 | 0.54 | 0.81 | 0.89 | 0.56 | 1.00 |

**Notes:** REERJ = Aggregate REER based on trade partner's export weights; REER1 = Clothing Industry—specific REER based on Competitor group 1 weights; REER2 = Clothing Industry—specific REER based on Competitor group 2 weights; REER3 = Clothing Industry—specific REER based on Competitor group 3 weights; REER4 = Clothing Industry—specific REER based on Competitor group 4 weights; Competitor group 1 weights are all the countries in Table 5.3 and groups 2, 3, and 4 correspond to the countries in groups 2, 3, and 4 in endnote 10.

## Econometric Results

The pooled regression results for Jamaica, Barbados, Costa Rica and the Dominican Republic for the period 1968–1988 are presented in Table 5.6. The individual country results are presented in Tables 5.7, 5.8, 5.9, and 5.10. The estimation procedure is OLS and the sample period is 1968–1988. However, as stated earlier, the individual country results are *only* presented for REER and REER1 as these are the most important weights, and for the remaining REERs the results are footnoted.

The REER variable performs reasonably well in the pooled model. It is statistically significant at 10% and the elasticities are 1.08 and 0.75 for REER and REER1, respectively. One would expect the elasticity to be greater than 1 to suggest that an adjustment in the REER would stimulate a strong export supply response; but the pooled evidence is only partially in support of this.

In Table 5.6 the capital stock variable and the CU index are significant at 10% or better in both cases. In the case of the capital stock, given the crude nature of the variable, one has to be extremely cautious in interpreting the behavior of the variable, despite its encouraging performance.

An F-test of the restricted pooled model versus the unrestricted pooled model was done where the null hypothesis is the restricted model.[16] Since F-values were only calculated for both equations and given F-values of 20.19 and 11.16, respectively, one has to reject the null hypothesis of the restricted model indicating that pooling these countries might not be justified.

In summary, the pooled model performs reasonably well. The REER variable is significant in most cases and alternative weighting schemes do appear to affect the behavior of the variable significantly. The capital stock variable is significant at 10% or better but the results must be interpreted cautiously. The capacity utilization measure for the manufacturing sector is consistently significant at 10% or better, indicating that domestic demand pressure has a negative impact on clothing export supply in Caribbean-type economies.

The individual country results are quite good except possibly in the case of Costa Rica. The model performs particularly well in the Dominican Republic. The REER variable is significant at least once in each of the countries and perform best in the Dominican Republic and Costa Rica. Only the REER with aggregate export weights (i.e., REER) is significant in Jamaica and only with group 1 weights (REER1) is significant in Barbados. The elasticities are generally close to 1 or greater than 1 when the REER is significant, except in the case of Costa Rica for REER1.

The capital stock variable is significant at 10% or better in Barbados, Jamaica, and the Dominican Republic in both equations. The variable does not perform well in Costa Rica. Once again given the crude nature of the variable, one must be cautious in interpreting the elasticities and overall performance of the variable.

**Table 5.6**
**Pooled Regression Results Clothing Export Supply Equation (1968–1988)**
(t-ratio in parenthesis)
Note: All variables are in Log's[11]

| Equation | Constant | LOG REER | LOG REER1 | LOG K | LOG CUM | D1 | D2 | D3 | $R^2$ | $R^2$ | D.F | F-stat |
|---|---|---|---|---|---|---|---|---|---|---|---|---|
| (1) | 13.78 (4.30) *** | 1.08 (1.35) * | | 1.09 (3.44) *** | -2.61 (-3.38) *** | 1.97 (3.69) *** | 0.70 (0.87) | 4.74 (8.0) *** | 0.71 | 0.69 | 77 | 31.19 |
| (2) | 17.88 (5.96) *** | | 0.75 (1.4) * | 0.98 (3.41) *** | -2.53 (-3.54) *** | -0.81 (-1.33) * | -1.02 (-1.45) * | -0.33 (-0.55) | 0.33 | 0.29 | 77 | 4.91 |

**Notes:** All t-tests are one-tailed tests; Equation 1: REER using aggregate export weights (REER); Equation 2: REER using competitor group 1 weights (REER1); ***Means significant at 1% or better; **Means significant at 5% or better; *Means significant at 10% or better.

**Table 5.7**
**Barbados's Clothing Export Supply Equation[12] (1968–1988) (t-ratio in parentheses)**

| Constant | LOG REER | LOG REER1 | LOG K | LOG CUM | $R^2$ | $R^2$ | RHO[1] | n | D.W. | F-STAT |
|---|---|---|---|---|---|---|---|---|---|---|
| 4.99 (0.56) | 0.25 (0.35) | | 1.16 (1.34) * | -1.39 (-1.33) * | 0.94 | 0.92 | 0.77 (5.67) *** | 20 | 1.99 | 54.13 |
| 0.17 (0.03) | | 0.97 (2.00) *** | 3.09 (7.83) *** | -2.05 (-1.43) * | -0.92 | 0.91 | | 21 | 1.00 | 65.52 |

**Notes:** [1]RHO is the AR(1) coefficient. Serial correlation is corrected for via the Cochrane-Orcutt procedure;
All t-tests are one-tailed tests; ***Means significant at 1% or better; **Means significant at 5% or better; *Means significant at 10% or better.

**Table 5.8**
**Jamaica's Clothing Export Supply Equation[13] (1968–1988) (t-ratio in parentheses)**

| Constant | LOG REER | LOG REER1 | LOG K | LOG CUM | $R^2$ | $R^2$ | n | D.W. | F-STAT |
|---|---|---|---|---|---|---|---|---|---|
| 8.02 (1.49) * | 2.73 (2.77) *** | | 1.22 (3.79) *** | 1.13 (2.11) | 0.85 | 0.83 | 21 | 1.58 | 32.78 |
| -4.16 (-1.14) | | 0.14 (0.32) | 1.86 (7.01) *** | 0.19 (0.37) | 0.79 | 0.75 | 21 | 1.06 | 20.97 |

**Notes:** All t-tests are one-tailed tests; ***Means significant at 1% or better; **Means significant at 5% or better; *Means significant at 10% or better.

**Table 5.9**
**Costa Rica's Clothing Export Supply Equation[14] (1968–1988) (t-ratio in parentheses)**

| Constant | LOG REER | LOG REER1 | LOG K | LOG CUM | $R^2$ | $R^2$ | Rho[1] | n | D.W. | F-STAT |
|---|---|---|---|---|---|---|---|---|---|---|
| 26.97 (6.83) *** | 4.77 (3.74) *** | | 0.19 (0.51) | 0.59 (0.73) | 0.61 | 0.54 | | 21 | 1.17 | 8.83 |
| 11.05 (7.52) *** | | 0.45 (1.60) * | -0.47 (-1.72) | 0.97 (2.02) | 0.93 | 0.91 | 0.72 (10.13) *** | 20 | 2.07 | 50.64 |

**Notes:** [1]Rho is the AR(1) Coefficient. Serial correlation is corrected for via the Cochrane-Orcutt procedure. All t-tests are one-tailed tests. ***Means significant at 1% or better; **Means significant at 5% or better; *Means significant at 10% or better.

**Table 5.10**

**Dominican Republic's Clothing Export Supply Equation[15] (1968–1988) (t-ratio in parentheses)**

| Constant | LOG REER | LOG REER1 | LOG K | LOG CUM | $R^2$ | $R^2$ | n | D.W. | F-STAT |
|---|---|---|---|---|---|---|---|---|---|
| 14.72 (2.71) *** | 9.18 (11.74) *** | | 6.12 (15.82) *** | -3.36 (-2.52) ** | 0.96 | 0.94 | 21 | 1.74 | 111.33 |
| 25.47 (2.66) *** | | 4.38 (5.57) *** | 3.77 (6.21) *** | -6.46 (2.89) *** | 0.84 | 0.82 | 21 | 1.15 | 30.57 |

**Notes:** All t-tests are one-tailed tests; ***Means significant at 1% or better; **Means significant at 5% or better; *Means significant at 10% or better.

The capacity utilization variable performs well in the Dominican Republic and Barbados. In the case of Jamaica and Costa Rica the variable is not statistically significant. In short, the results for the proxy for domestic demand pressure are mixed.

In summary, the individual country results, like the pooled ones, point to the likelihood that exchange rate depreciation or changes in incentives will have a positive impact on clothing exports. In addition, the behavior of the REER variable differs depending on the set of country weights that are used. The performance of the capital stock variable is encouraging but the results must be interpreted cautiously. Finally, the performance of the capacity utilization index is mixed and is not significant in Jamaica and Costa Rica. The performance of the variable might improve if one had a capacity utilization measure that related specifically to the export sector.

### 5.3c  Industry-Specific Export Equation: Miscellaneous Manufactures

Other nontraditional exports that were sold mainly to non-CARICOM markets over the period 1968–1988 were miscellaneous manufactures (SITC 89).

In Barbados, clothing, electronics and miscellaneous manufactures were the main exports to non-CARICOM markets in the period. During the 1979–1988 period electronics exports boosted manufactured exports significantly. They represented at least 25% of total manufactured exports in 1979 and 60% by 1987. The rapid growth in electronic exports was largely due to the operation of a large INTEL electronics plant in the period 1979–1987. When INTEL shut its doors in 1987 electronic exports collapsed.

In Jamaica clothing exports to the United States dominated the manufactured export basket in the 1980s, commanding at least 70% of total manufactured exports. Despite the relatively small share of miscellaneous manufactures in total manufactured exports, they were in fact, the second largest nontraditional export to non-CARICOM markets in the period.

The data in Table 5.11a indicate the sharply declining importance of miscellaneous manufactured exports in total manufactured exports and the importance of the U.S. market for Jamaica and Barbados. Tables 5.11a and 5.11b show that miscellaneous manufactures became less important to total manufactured exports and the U.S. market declined in importance in the 1980s. The declining share of miscellaneous manufactures in Barbados can be explained by the relatively fast growth of electronic exports from 1978. In Jamaica the rapid growth in clothing exports far outstripped the growth in miscellaneous manufactures and thus reduced their share of total manufactured exports.

The declining importance of the U.S. market was due largely to the rising share of exports to Trinidad and Tobago by both Jamaica and Barbados. In the period 1976–1983 Trinidad and Tobago experienced a substantial growth in

| Table 5.11a<br>Share of Miscellaneous Manufactured Exports in<br>Total Manufactured Exports: Jamaica and Barbados | | | |
|---|---|---|---|
| Country | 1968 | 1979 | 1987 |
| Barbados | 35% | 10% | 15% |
| Jamaica | 10% | 3% | 3% |

**Source:** Calculated from U.N. Commodity Trade Statistics.

| Table 5.11b<br>Exports to the U.S. as a Percentage of Total Miscellaneous<br>Manufactured Exports: Jamaica and Barbados | | | |
|---|---|---|---|
| Country | 1968 | 1979 | 1987 |
| Barbados | 85% | 63% | 20% |
| Jamaica | 39% | 25% | 25% |

**Source:** Calculated from U.N. Commodity Trade Statistics.

**Note:** Costa Rica and the Dominican Republic are omitted from the tables because their exports of miscellaneous manufactures to the United States are negligible.

export earnings resulting from increased receipts from oil exports. A lot of CARICOM manufacturers found it easier to shift their attention away from attempting increased penetration of the U.S., or other developed country markets, to expanding sales to Trinidad and Tobago during the period of unprecedented growth in import spending financed by the oil windfall. Recent discussions with officials at export promotion organizations in Jamaica and Barbados indicate that with the rapid decline in Trinidad and Tobago's economy since 1984, manufactures have once again begun to concentrate their attention on trying to penetrate the U.S. market.

Guyana and Trinidad and Tobago were omitted once again, as miscellaneous manufactures were a negligible percentage of their total manufactured exports. Furthermore, manufactured exports are a relatively small percentage of total merchandise exports in Trinidad and Tobago and Guyana (see Table 5.12). The increase in the share from 6% in 1979 to 25% in 1988 in Trinidad and Tobago was largely due to the growth in some "new" capital intensive industries—ammonia, urea, fertilizers, methanol, and steel rods—that were developed from the proceeds of the oil windfall.

A similar model as before is used for the estimation of an export supply equation for miscellaneous manufactures. The only modification is to the weights used in calculating the competitor-weighted REER.

| Table 5.12 The Share of Manufactured Exports in Total Merchandise Exports: Selected Caribbean Countries | | | |
|---|---|---|---|
| Country | 1968 | 1979 | 1988 |
| Guyana | 4% | 6% | 14% |
| Trinidad and Tobago | 13% | 6% | 25% |
| Barbados | 17% | 61% | 48% |
| Jamaica | 9% | 52% | 65% |

**Source:** Calculated from the *World Tables* (1989-1990 edition).

As argued previously, U.S. producers and other developed country suppliers are not included in the set of competitor weights. In determining the set of unconstrained developing country suppliers the attempt was made to devise a list of developing countries (for which data were available) that did not face quotas, voluntary export restraints, or any other barrier to entry. It was extremely difficult to obtain such detailed information, and this research was complicated more by the wide range of products that are classified as miscellaneous manufactures. The decision made was to omit developing countries that are known to face barriers to entry in the U.S. market for their exports (e.g., east Asian NIEs—Taiwan, Korea, Hong Kong, Singapore—Brazil, and India). It was recognized that this was not a particularly persuasive criterion but it is difficult to improve upon, given the difficulties of disentangling the U.S. trade regime for the range of commodities classified as miscellaneous manufactures. As a result of these exercises the following list of countries was arrived at:

### Group 5[17]

| | |
|---|---|
| Mexico | Pakistan |
| Haiti | Malaysia |
| Venezuela | Indonesia |
| Barbados | Philippines |
| Jamaica | Thailand |

The correlation coefficients for Jamaica and Barbados between the REER based on aggregate export weights and Group 5 weights are 0.80 in both cases. The correlation coefficients are high, suggesting that the alternative weighting schemes are not significantly affecting the measurement of the variable.

The capital stock data and the measure of capacity utilization are identical to those used in the clothing export supply equation. Therefore, the estimating equation is the following:

$$logMISCXC = C_0 + C_1 \, logREER + C_2 \, logK + C_3 \, logCU.$$

$$C_1 > 0; \quad C_2 > 0; \quad C_3 < 0.$$

Where:

| | | |
|---|---|---|
| MISCXC | = | Miscellaneous manufactures (constant price)[18] |
| REER | = | Using aggregate export weights and group 5 weights |

### Econometric Results

The pooled results are presented in Table 5.13 and the results for Jamaica and Barbados are presented in Table 5.14. The pooled results are definitely not encouraging. The real effective exchange rate variable is not statistically significant at 10% or better. The capital stock and capacity utilization variables are also not statistically significant and the overall explanatory power of the regression is weak with a low $R^2$.

The possibility that the weak performance of the independent variables might be due to the presence of multicollinearity was investigated. However, the Farrar-Glauber equations for the pooled equation had $R^2$ ranging from 0.30 to 0.75 and did not suggest the presence of multicollinearity.

The poor performance of the real effective exchange rate variable might be due to the unavoidable lack of rigor in determining the set of competitor countries (Group 5) to be used as weights. In addition, the crude nature of the capital stock variable might be affecting its performance.

The results for Jamaica and Barbados show no improvement in the performance. The real effective exchange rate variable is not significant at 10% or better, irrespective of the weights used. The capital stock variable is significant at 10% or better in Jamaica but it is not significant in Barbados. The capacity utilization index is not significant in both countries.

The possibility of the presence of multicollinearity was investigated. In the case of Barbados the partial correlation coefficient between REER5 and K is −0.96. Furthermore, the $R^2$ from the Farrar-Glauber equations is 0.92. There is thus evidence of the presence of multicollinearity in Barbados affecting the results. One possible alternative with the presence of multicollinearity is pooling. But as I reported earlier the pooled results are not encouraging. In the case of Jamaica the partial correlation coefficient is 0.54 and the $R^2$ is 0.40. Thus, there does not appear to be the presence of multicollinearity in Jamaica.

In summary, the overall results suggest that the equation is not well estimated. The presence of harmful multicollinearity in Barbados affected the performance of the model. One might argue that the crude nature of the independent variables might be affecting the model. Alternatively, it is possible that in this case the model is mis-specified.

## Table 5.13
### Pooled Regression Results: Miscellaneous Manufactures (1968–1988) (t-statistics in parentheses)

| Equation | Constant | LOG REER[1] | LOG REER5[2] | LOG K | LOG CUM | $R^2$ | $R^2$ | n | F-STAT | D1 |
|---|---|---|---|---|---|---|---|---|---|---|
| (1) | -9.70 (-2.09) ** | -2.03 (-2.63) | | -0.08 (0.19) | -0.01 (0.01) | 0.32 | 0.18 | 42 | 3.01 | 0.54 (0.88) |
| (2) | -5.30 | | 0.8 (0.83) | 0.26 (0.63) | 1.15 (1.39) * | 0.19 | 0.08 | 42 | 1.72 | 0.04 (0.07) |

**Notes:** [1]REER based on aggregate export weights; [2]REER5 based on Group 5 competitor weights; All t-tests are one-tailed tests; ***Means significant at 1% or better; **Means significant at 5% or better; *Means significant at 10% or better.

132

## Table 5.14
### Jamaica and Barbados Export Supply Equation (1968–1988)
### Dependent Variable: Miscellaneous Manufactures (t-statistics in parentheses)

| Equation | Constant | LOG REER | LOG REER5 | LOG K | LOG CUM | $R^2$ | $\bar{R}^2$ | n | D.W. | F-STAT | RHO |
|---|---|---|---|---|---|---|---|---|---|---|---|
| (1) | 36.25 1.92 ** | 1.57 (0.75) | | 0.42 (0.35) | -5.54 (-1.33) * | 0.54 | 0.49 | 20 | 1.49 | 5.32 | 0.76 (4.25) *** |
| (2) | 8.95 (0.60) | | -1.45 (-1.15) | -1.71 (-0.90) | 0.01 0.01 | 0.64 | 0.52 | 20 | 1.04 | 5.86 | 0.79 (4.10) *** |
| (3) | -10.11 (-0.99) | -0.97 (-0.52) | | 1.05 (1.73) ** | 1.10 (1.08) | 0.24 | 0.11 | 21 | 1.03 | 1.81 | |
| (4) | -18.512 (-1.62) * | | 1.59 (1.27) | 1.64 (2.20) ** | 0.82 (0.90) | 0.23 | 0.14 | 21 | 1.22 | 2.10 | |

**Notes:** Equations (1) and (2) are Barbados; Equations (3) and (4) are for Jamaica; Rho is the AR (1) coefficient; Equations (1) and (2) were corrected for first-order serial correlation; All t-tests are one-tailed tests; ***Means significant at 1% or better; **Means significant at 5% or better; *Means significant at 10% or better.

133

## 5.4 AGGREGATE EXPORTS

The conventional export supply model is also applied to total real merchandise exports.[19] The only real effective exchange rate variable that is used is the one that is based on aggregate export weights (i.e., REER). The capacity utilization index is now calculated using economywide GDP value not added in manufacturing. The pooled results are presented in Table 5.14 and the individual country results in Table 5.15. Note that the sample period is 1968–1989, since additional data for 1989 is available for aggregate exports. The pooled regression results are reasonably good. Both the REER and capital stock variables are statistically significant and the former's elasticity is 0.6. The CU variable is not significant at 10% or better.

The results for aggregate real exports at the country level are mixed. The REER variable is significant at 10% or better only in Trinidad and Tobago, and the export supply elasticity is 0.75. The REER variable is not significant in Jamaica, Guyana, and Barbados. It might be that the increased aggregation in exports is affecting the performance of the variable. Note for instance that aggregate exports include sugar which is quota-constrained.

The capital stock variable is significant at 10% or better in Trinidad and Tobago and Guyana but is not significant in Jamaica. The capacity utilization variable has the correct sign in Trinidad and Tobago and Barbados but is not statistically significant. In short, the individual country results do not indicate (except in Trinidad and Tobago) that altering incentives will increase export supply, but the increased aggregation in exports is probably affecting the results.

It would be useful to compare the performance of the model with other countries that are similar to the Caribbean to examine the extent to which the results are consistent with those in Table 5.17. The decision rule for choosing countries was as follows: GNP per capita in 1989 of US$426 or more, small size (population less than 7 million), and manufacturing accounting for at least 20% of GDP. This rule lead us to choose Costa Rica, the Dominican Republic (a non-CARICOM Caribbean country), and Mauritius, each of which also had data available (from the same sources) for the period 1968–1989. Note, this is the same period for which data are available for the Caribbean countries. The results for these countries are presented in Table 5.17.

The results in Table 5.17 are not really similar to those for the CARICOM countries, given that the REER variable is significant at 10% or better in all three countries, opposite the case for the CARICOM countries. The elasticity in Mauritius is 1.86 compared to 0.25 and 1.11 in the Dominican Republic and Costa Rica, respectively.

The capital stock variable does not perform as well in these countries. Only in the Dominican Republic is the variable significant with the correct sign. The crude nature of the variable might be affecting its performance in this case.

### Table 5.15
#### Pooled Regression Results for Total Export Supply Equation (1968–1989)
#### Dependent Variable: Real Merchandise Exports (t-statistics in parentheses)

| | LOG REER | LOG K | LOG Cu | D1 | D2 | D3 | $R^2$ | $R^2$ | n | F-STAT |
|---|---|---|---|---|---|---|---|---|---|---|
| Constant | 0.60 | 0.97 | 0.56 | 0.46 | 0.03 | 0.11 | 0.64 | 0.61 | 88 | 23.73 |
| 0.73 | (2.05) | (9.19) | (1.23) | (2.18) | (0.34) | (0.46) | | | | |
| (0.31) | ** | *** | | ** | | | | | | |

**Notes:** All t-tests are one-tailed tests; The base country is Barbados so that the intercept dummies are deviations from Barbados' intercept; An F-test of the restricted pooled model versus the unrestricted pooled model indicated that with a value of 1.19 one can accept the null hypothesis of the restricted model; ***Means significant at 1% or better; **Means significant at 5% or better; *Means significant at 10% or better.

### Table 5.16
#### Regression Results for Total Export Supply Equation for Some CARICOM Countries
#### Dependent Variable: Real Merchandise Exports (t-statistics in parentheses)

| Equation | Constant | LOG REER | LOG K | LOG Cu | $R^2$ | $R^2$ | n | D.W. | F-STAT | Rho |
|---|---|---|---|---|---|---|---|---|---|---|
| Trinidad and Tobago | 8.91 | 0.75 | -0.11 | 0.61 | 0.96 | 0.95 | 21 | 1.90 | 105.58 | 0.96 |
| | (4.62) | (2.11) | (-0.51) | (1.24) | | | | | | (12.72) |
| | *** | ** | | | | | | | | *** |
| Guyana | 7.63 | 0.14 | 0.16 | -0.39 | 0.40 | 0.30 | 22 | 1.17 | 8.80 | |
| | (6.19) | (0.94) | (1.44) | (-2.72) | | | | | | |
| | *** | | * | *** | | | | | | |
| Jamaica | 5.75 | -0.35 | -0.18 | 0.17 | 0.71 | 0.66 | 22 | 1.31 | 14.50 | |
| | (4.02) | (-1.22) | (-1.98) | (1.0) | | | | | | |
| | *** | | | | | | | | | |
| Barbados | -21.62 | -1.45 | 2.19 | 1.40 | 0.84 | 0.80 | 21 | 2.08 | 21.39 | 0.88 |
| | (-2.89) | (-2.53) | (3.72) | (1.11) | | | | | | (21.46) |
| | *** | *** | *** | | | | | | | *** |

**Notes:** All t-tests are one-tailed tests; ***Means significant at 1% or better; **Means significant at 5% or better; *Means significant at 10% or better.

**Table 5.17**

**Aggregate Export Supply Equation for Costa Rica, Dominican Republic and Mauritius (1968–1989) (t-statistics in parentheses)**

| Equation | Constant | LOG REER | LOG K | LOG Cu | $R^2$ | $R^2$ | n | D.W. | Rho | F-STAT |
|---|---|---|---|---|---|---|---|---|---|---|
| Dominican Republic | 7.51 (6.49) *** | 0.25 (2.03) ** | 0.22 (2.83) *** | -0.23 (-0.83) | 0.37 | 0.26 | 22 | 1.48 | | 3.28 |
| Costa Rica | 10.25 (14.65) ** | 1.11 (4.54) *** | 0.07 (1.11) | 0.25 (1.47) | 0.64 | 0.57 | 22 | 1.34 | | 9.58 |
| Mauritius | 7.28 (2.53) ** | 1.86 (2.91) *** | 0.10 (0.49) | 1.54 (2.97) | 0.76 | 0.69 | 21 | 1.96 | 0.56 (2.95) *** | 10.83 |

**Notes:** All t-tests are one-tailed tests; \*\*\*Means significant at 1% or better; \*\*Means significant at 5% or better; \*Means significant at 10% or better.

Finally, the capacity utilization index has the correct sign in the Dominican Republic but is not significant.

In summary, the REER variable performs reasonably well in the latter set of countries. The performance of the capital stock and capacity utilization variables is mixed, but the former might be affected by the crude nature of the variable. The poor performance of Caribbean exports over the last two decades is a source of great concern to policymakers. This chapter uses a partial model of export supply to isolate some of the key determinants of the Caribbean's export performance. The results would seem to suggest that exchange rate depreciation and/or incentives that increase the relative profitability of tradable production have a positive impact on the performance of some nontraditional exports and to a lesser extent overall exports. It was not possible to analyze the effects of other incentives but a previous chapter addressed some of these issues. The challenge for policymakers is to formulate a package of incentives (which must be maintained over time) to stimulate tradable production. In addition, productive capacity generally has a positive impact on exports, but we must interpret the results cautiously given the crude nature of the "proxy." Finally, domestic demand pressure effects vary to some degree across countries. The performance of the variable might improve if we had a sector specific measure.

## NOTES

1. Caribbean countries referred to here are specifically the members of the Caribbean community (CARICOM), which are all thirteen English-speaking Caribbean countries.

2. There are two unpublished papers—Cox and Worrell (1979) and Ramcharan (1983)—which employ "export functions" but these are not conventional export supply functions. Ramcharan's formulation is the following:

$$Q_x = f(P_x, Y) .$$

Where:

$Q_x$    =    Real exports
$P_x$    =    Export price index
$Y$     =    Real GDP of the exporting country

Cox and Worrell (1979) alter the equation using relative prices instead of $P_x$ alone.

3. This is to make it plain that the relationship between quantities and prices is, at least in theory, simultaneous.

4. Goldstein and Khan (1984) cite three reasons advanced in the literature for a divergence between domestic prices and export prices: (1)Different demand elasticities in the home export market; (2)different cost structures for home and export production; or, (3) simply distortions in the market.

5. Faini (1988) also alludes to the difficulty of obtaining data for the purposes of building a satisfactory indicator of the "effective" (i.e., subsidy corrected) price of exports.

6. Nontraditional exports are defined in the Caribbean as all exports except for the major primary exports and tourism.

7. An important aspect of the U.S. trade regime is the "807" import program. The essence of the program is that when a country exports products made of, at least in part, certain U.S. components, the value of the U.S. components is exempt from U.S. customs duties under the U.S. Tariff Schedule, line 807.0.

8. The coverage of clothing export data is not consistent across different sources. In particular, Caribbean export data do not accord with US import data. The differences are particularly noticeable in the 1970s and in Costa Rica, in particular from among the countries in the sample.

9. The arrangement regarding international trade in textiles, better known as the Multi-Fibre Arrangement (MFA) came into effect on January 1, 1974. The underlying principle of the MFA was the need for some sort of organization in the international trade of all textiles. It sought to legitimize the quotas that the industrialized countries were increasingly placing on imports of cotton, synthetic and wool textiles from the producing nations. Just as with previous arrangements it attempted to share the burden of increased imports more evenly among importers.

10. This group of unconstrained suppliers was divided into three groups:

**Group 2 (Central America and the Caribbean)**
Jamaica
Barbados
Honduras
Guatemala
El Salvador
**Group 3 (Latin America)**
Argentina
Peru
Uruguay
Bolivia
**Group 4 (The Rest)**
Malta
Mauritius
Turkey
Morocco

These three groups, plus group 1, are used as weights in calculating the REER to be used in estimating the pooled and individual country clothing export supply equation. The REER based on aggregate export weights is also used. Therefore, five equations are estimated each corresponding to an REER with a different weight. The list of REERs are as follows:

REER　　=　　aggregate export weights
REER1　=　　using set of unconstrained suppliers to the U.S. markets. (see Table 5.3)
REER2　=　　using Group 2 weights
REER3　=　　using Group 3 weights
REER4　=　　using Group 4 weights

11. See Table 5.18 on page 139.
12. See Table 5.19 on page 140.
13. See Table 5.20 on page 141.
14. See Table 5.21 on page 142.

## Table 5.18
### Pooled Regression Results Clothing Export Supply Equation (1968–1988): Alternative Competitor-Group Weights (t-ratio in parentheses)

| Equation | Constant | LOG REER2 | LOG REER3 | LOG REER4 | LOG K | LOG CUM | 0 | D2 | D3 | $R^2$ | $R^2$ | D.F. | F-stat |
|---|---|---|---|---|---|---|---|---|---|---|---|---|---|
| (1) | 17.20 (5.77) *** | 0.62 (1.04) | | | 1.03 (3.53) *** | -2.60 (-3.60) *** | -0.82 (-1.33) * | -0.91 (-1.30) | -0.54 (-0.94) | 0.32 | 0.28 | 80 | 4.72 |
| (2) | 15.04 (6.24) ** | | 1.23 (3.90) *** | | 0.89 (3.32) *** | -1.30 (-1.74) ** | -0.54 (-0.93) | -0.77 (-1.21) | 0.04 (0.07) | 0.44 | 0.41 | 80 | 8.01 |
| (3) | 14.20 (4.11) *** | | | -0.44 (-0.67) | 0.94 (3.09) *** | -2.92 (-4.31) *** | -0.84 (-1.35) * | -0.77 (-1.07) | -0.46 (-0.81) | 0.30 | 0.27 | 80 | 4.61 |

**Notes:** Equation 1: Competitor group 2 weights (REER2); Equation 2: Competitor group 3 weights (REER3); Equation 3: Competitor group 4 weights (REER4); ***Means significant at 1% or better; **Means significant at 5% or better; *Means significant at 10% or better.

## Table 5.19
### Barbados's Clothing Export Supply Equation (1968–1988): Alternative Competitor Group Weights (t-ratio in parentheses)

| Constant | LOG REER2 | LOG REER3 | LOG REER4 | LOG K | LOG CUM | $R^2$ | $R^2$ | n | D.W. | F-STAT |
|---|---|---|---|---|---|---|---|---|---|---|
| -0.77 (-0.11) | 0.45 (1.06) | | | 2.73 (7.24) *** | -1.94 (-1.23) | 0.91 | 0.89 | 21 | 1.09 | 55.75 |
| 3.41 (0.42) | | -0.06 (-0.27) | | 1.26 (1.45) * | -1.50 (-1.16) | 0.94 | 0.92 | 21 | 1.88 | 54.02 |
| -3.28 (-0.65) | | | 1.67 (4.09) *** | 3.81 (10.16) *** | -1.50 (1.31) * | 0.95 | 0.94 | 21 | 1.37 | 108.71 |

## Table 5.20
### Jamaica's Clothing Export Supply Equation (1968–1988):
### Alternative Competitor Group Weights (t-ratio in parentheses)

| Constant | LOG REER2 | LOG REER3 | LOG REER4 | LOG K | LOG CUM | $R^2$ | $R^2$ | n | D.W. | F-STAT |
|---|---|---|---|---|---|---|---|---|---|---|
| -5.20 (-1.35) * | -0.21 (-0.36) | | | 1.87 (7.06) *** | 0.05 (0.09) | 0.79 | 0.75 | 21 | 1.09 | 21.01 |
| -5.07 (-1.27) | | -0.06 (-0.19) | | 2.03 (5.63) *** | -0.10 (-0.19) | 0.83 | 0.79 | 21 | 1.97 | 25.35 |
| -2.64 (-0.59) | | | 0.44 (0.67) | 1.86 (7.09) *** | 0.16 (0.34) | 0.79 | 0.75 | 21 | 1.02 | 21.52 |

**Table 5.21**

**Costa Rica's Clothing Export Supply Equation (1968–1988):**
**Alternative Competitor Group Weights (t-ratio in parentheses)**

| Constant | LOG REER2 | LOG REER3 | LOG REER4 | LOG K | LOG CUM | $R^2$ | $R^2$ | Rho | D.W. | n | F-STAT |
|---|---|---|---|---|---|---|---|---|---|---|---|
| 10.64 (7.08) *** | 0.53 (1.85) ** | | | -0.68 (-2.10) | 1.48 (2.27) * | 0.93 | 0.91 | 0.72 ((10.67) *** | 2.21 | 20 | 44.27 |
| 9.84 (6.88) *** | | -0.04 ((-0.01) | | -0.54 (-1.86) | 0.91 (1.75) | 0.92 | 0.90 | 0.72 (9.67) *** | 2.08 | 20 | 42.68 |
| 10.88 (6.28) *** | | | 0.29 (0.88) | -0.57 (-2.12) | 1.09 (2.03) | 0.92 | 0.90 | 0.71 (9.65) *** | 2.07 | 20 | 45.01 |

**Notes:** All t-tests are one-tailed tests; ***Means significant at 1% or better; **Means significant at 5% or better; *Means significant at 10% or better.

## Table 5.22
### Dominican Republic's Clothing Export Supply Equation (1968–1988): Alternative Competitor Group Weights (t-ratio in parentheses)

| Constant | LOG REER2 | LOG REER3 | LOG REER4 | LOG K | LOG CUM | R² | R² | n | D.W. | F-STAT | Rho |
|---|---|---|---|---|---|---|---|---|---|---|---|
| 45.77 (2.93) *** | 4.31 (2.40) ** | | | 3.11 (3.39) *** | -9.68 (-3.16) *** | 0.67 | 0.61 | 21 | 1.08 | 11.50 | |
| 25.60 (2.23) ** | | 2.55 (4.05) *** | | 3.34 (4.51) *** | -7.27 (-2.73) *** | 0.77 | 0.74 | 21 | 1.00 | 19.57 | |
| 12.17 (0.92) | | | 1.75 (1.30) * | 1.55 (0.90) | -0.58 (-0.36) | 0.96 | 0.95 | 20 | 2.22 | 90.56 | 0.96 ((10.72) *** |

143

15. See Table 5.22 on page 143.

16. The following F-statistic was calculated:

$$F\,[k_y \sum N{-}jk] = \frac{\{\,SSR_{(P)} - (\sum SSR\,)\}\Big/ \begin{matrix}(N_{1+N_2}-k)\\-[(N_1-k)+(N_2-k)]\end{matrix}}{(\sum SSR)/(N_1+N_2-2k)}\,,$$

where:

| | | |
|---|---|---|
| SSR$_P$ | = | Residual sum of squares pooled regression |
| N | = | no. of observations |
| j | = | no. of countries |
| k | = | no. of parameters |
| $\Sigma$N | = | total number of observations. |

17. This means that the following group of countries have been excluded from the set of competitor counties:

**Excluded Countries**
Argentina
Brazil
Colombia
India
Peru
Ecuador*
Uruguay*
Monaco*
Bahamas*

*These countries were excluded because of missing data points in the period 1968–1988. In other words, they were present in U.S. import data in some years and absent in others.

18. Deflated by the export price index (1980–100).

19. The model was also applied to real merchandise exports plus tourist receipts and real tourist receipts. In both cases the performance of the model was similar. Notably, there was no significant change in the supply elasticity of the real effective exchange rate variable.

## APPENDIX 5.A.1
## THE IMPERFECT SUBSTITUTES MODEL

Following Goldstein and Khan (1984) in equations (1) through (8) below, we present a "bare-bones" imperfect substitutes model of country $I$'s imports from and exports to the rest of the world. (This is, of course, the supply of exports of the rest of the world to country $i$.)

$$I_i^d = f(Y_i, PI_i, P_i), f_1, f_3 > 0, f_2 < 0, \tag{1}$$

$$X_i^d = g(Y*e, PX_i, P*e), g_1, g_3 > 0, g_2 < 0, \tag{2}$$

$$I_i^s = h[PI*(1+s*), P*], h_1 > 0, h_2 < 0, \tag{3}$$

$$X_i^s = j[PX_i(1+s_i), P_i] \, j_1 > 0, j_2 < 0, \tag{4}$$

$$PI_i = PX*(1+T_i) \, e, \tag{5}$$

$$PI* = PX_i(1+T*)/e, \tag{6}$$

$$I_i^d = I_i^s e, \tag{7}$$

$$X_i^d = S_i^s. \tag{8}$$

These eight equations determine the quantity of imports demanded in country $i$ ($I_i^d$), the quantity of country $i$'s exports demanded by the rest of the world ($X_i^d$), the quantity of imports supplied to country $i$ from the rest of the world ($I_i^s$)[1], the quantity of exports supplied from country $i$ to the rest of the world ($X_i^s$), the domestic currency prices paid by importers in the two regions ($PI_i$ and $PI*$), and the domestic currency prices received by exporters in two regions ($PX_i$, $PX*$). The exogenous variables are the levels of nominal income in the two regions ($Y_i, Y*$), the price of (all) domestically produced goods in the two regions ($P_i, P*$), the proportional tariff ($T_i, T*$) and subsidy rates ($S_i, S*$) applied to imports and exports in the two regions, and the exchange rate (e) linking the two currencies (expressed in units of country $I$'s currency per unit of the rest of the world's currency).

## APPENDIX 5.A.2
## THE DERIVATION OF CAPITAL STOCK ESTIMATES

$$I_t = K_t - K_{t-1} + \alpha K_{t-1}, \tag{1}$$

or,

$$I_t = K_t - (1-\alpha)K_{t-1}, \tag{2}$$

hence,

$$I_t = (1-\beta L)K_t,$$

where:

$$\beta = (1-\alpha),$$

so,

$$K_t = \frac{I_t}{(1-\beta L)}$$

$$K_t = \beta I_t + \beta^2 I_{t-1} + \beta^3 I_{t-2} +, \tag{3}$$

where:

| | | |
|---|---|---|
| $I_t$ | = | gross domestic investment |
| $K_t$ | = | capital stock |
| a | = | depreciation rate |

In calculating the capital stock two depreciation rates were used—5% and 10%. With two estimates of the capital stock one can test the sensitivity of the estimates to different depreciation rates in the estimation of the model. However, preliminary estimates of the model did not detect any sensitivity of the model to different estimates of the capital stock. So, a depreciation rate of 10% is used in deriving the capital stock estimates.

To obtain constant value 1980 dollar estimates of the capital stock in a common currency (US$), the approach adopted by Leamer (1984: 233) was followed and investment flows were converted year by year into dollars. The U.S. GDP deflator was used to convert to constant dollars.

**APPENDIX 5.A.3**
**PLOTS OF CLOTHING EXPORTS FOR THE U.S.**
**MARKET-SELECTED COUNTRIES (1968–1988)**

**Figure 5.1**
**Barbados's Clothing Exports to the United States (1968–1988; US$million)**

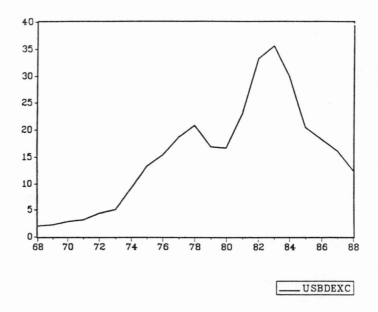

USBDEXC

**Figure 5.2**
**Dominican Republic's Clothing Exports to the United States (1968–1988; US$million)**

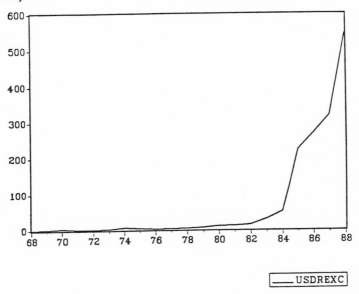

USDREXC

**Figure 5.3**
**Jamaica's Clothing Exports to the United States (1968–1988; US$million)**

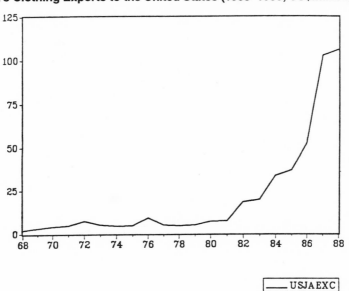

USJAEXC

**Figure 5.4**
**Costa Rica's Clothing Exports to the United States (1968–1988; US$million)**

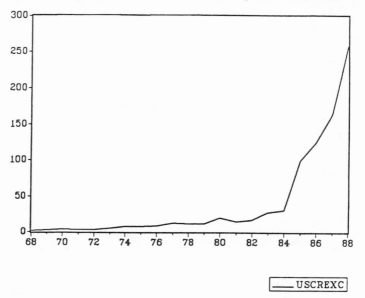

USCREXC

# 6

## The Regional Dimension

In analyzing the region's export performance and policies that have been deployed for the development of exports, one must include the regional integration experience. The regional integration strategy has been an important plank of development policy in CARICOM countries and national efforts at export promotion will have to be consistent with the policies of the integration strategy. This chapter analyzes the evolution of the integration model in CARICOM, identifying its salient factors over time. The influence or potential impact of official IMF/World Bank structural adjustment programs in the regional integration strategy is also analyzed. Finally, the role of the integration model in facilitating export promotion in the medium term is discussed.

### 6.1 CARICOM'S MODEL OF ECONOMIC INTEGRATION

The Caribbean community (CARICOM) was established in 1973 with the signing of the Treaty of Chaguaramas. The movement from CARIFTA (Caribbean Free Trade Association) to CARICOM was an important landmark in the integration movement among the English-speaking Caribbean countries. CARICOM is not solely a customs union. CARICOM is an economic integration movement (including cooperation) that has at its core the concept of production integration.

Early works on Caribbean economic integration espoused ideas of "resource combination" [McIntyre (1966)] and "structural transformation" [Demas (1965)]. McIntyre argued that Caribbean countries could overcome resource constraints by combining their natural resources to develop areas of export specialization (e.g., aluminum smelting). The development of new export activities utilizing regional resources was intended to reduce the region's dependence on traditional agricultural exports (e.g., bananas and sugar).

Building on these ideas Brewster and Thomas (1967) introduced the concept of "production integration" that essentially reformed to the "combination of natural resources and capital across the region in vertically-integrated, resource-based production for the satisfaction of demand in an integrated regional market, and/or for export production" [Girvan et al. (1993: 4)].

The concept of production integration was developed in the context of an economic strategy centered around national import-substituting industrialization (ISI), which was being pursued by CARICOM's more developed countries (MDCs) in the 1960s. At the national level, the ISI strategy had encountered two acute constraints: First, the limitations of small market size did not permit capacity expansion and economies of scale. Secondly, a heavy dependence on imported inputs that encouraged low-value added industries and limited employment generation. The creation of a customs union or market integration would reduce the constraint of small market size, the first major constraint, and production integration was supposed to address the second major constraint.

The concept of production integration was an integral part of the Treaty of Chaguaramas. This was manifested in several provisions of the treaty. Among the more important are the provision for regional industrial programming (Article 46), the provision for the joint development of natural resources (Article 47) and the Provision for the rationalization and integration of the agricultural sector (Article 49). An important feature of all of these key provisions of the treaty is that they all involve a high level of government involvement, either through government ownership or sponsorship of the initiatives.

## 6.1a  Regional Industrial Programming

Traditionally, economic integration schemes in developing countries have accorded a central role to the state in the integration process. This is clearly manifested by the state's involvement in projects of resource combination (e.g., aluminum smelting), industrial complementarity, and export specialization in the productive sectors, particularly industry and agriculture.

State guided production integration usually involves a scheme for regional industrial programming (RIP). Girvan et al. (1993: 12) in analyzing production integration efforts in CARICOM, argued that RIP involves two sets of activities:

1. government determination of the pattern and scope for production specialization within the area by the conduct of feasibility studies, social cost-benefit analysis, etc.; and

2. implementation of the desired changes in the production structure by a variety of instruments including tariffs, fiscal incentives, administrative controls, and investments by state enterprises.

In CARICOM, type (2) activities have been identified as the focus of RIP initiatives. There has been the formulation of intergovernmental agreements that allocated investments in new plants or industries to specific countries. Article 46 of the Treaty of Chaguaramas established the Caribbean Industrial Programming Scheme (CIPS). Under the mandate from Article 46 CIPS was designed to achieve the following objectives [see Girvan et al. (1993: 13)]:

a. the greater utilization of the raw materials of the Common Market;

b. the creation of production linkages both within and between the national economies of the Common Market;

c. to minimize product differentiation and achieve economies of large scale production, consistent with the limitations of market size;

d. the encouragement of greater efficiency in industrial production;

e. the promotion of exports to markets both within and outside the Common Market; and

f. an equitable distribution of the benefits of industrialization paying particular attention to the need to locate more industries in the Less developed countries (LDCs).

Given the above objectives and the natural resources base of CARICOM countries, the following activities were identified as technically feasible:

1. wood-based products: plywood, veneer, prefabricated houses, sashes and doors

2. clay-based ceramic products

3. fish processing

4. agroprocessing

5. chemical lime and chemical pulp

6. cotton textiles and textile products

7. leather products

8. plastic products

9. agricultural hand tools and other steel-based products

10. sugar-based products

11. petroleum-based products.

In 1986 the CARICOM heads of government conference approved the above list of activities as eligible for integrated production at the regional level. To date, no integrated industries have emerged and what little activity has occurred has been at the national level.

To meet the special needs of the LDCs, the Industrial Allocation Scheme was developed and certain light manufacturing industries were allocated to the LDCs. This scheme has also had no success and is no longer actively considered by CARICOM governments. Worrell argued that "no country was willing to withdraw benefits that existing industry enjoyed, even in areas where other CARICOM countries produced more competitively" (1994: 7). Apart from a few natural resource-based industries, such as petrochemicals in Trinidad and Tobago, few activities recommended themselves for location in one country rather than another.

Efforts to predetermine industrial location were misconceived. The decision of where to produce should have been guided by underlying economic factors related to comparative advantage or, more specifically, comparative costs of production. A more fruitful approach would have been to focus on creating the regional environment that would permit investors to pursue profitable opportunities (at the regional level). State involvement should have been restricted to providing technical assistance, export marketing support services, and finance to firms that were prepared to engage in export activities.

## 6.1b  Regional Agricultural Development

CARICOM attempted to some extent to program the development of the agricultural sector at the regional level. Under the mandate of Article 49 of the Treaty of Chaguaramas the following objectives were set for the scheme of regional agricultural development [see Girvan et al. (1993: 15)]:

1. the development of a regional plan for the integration of agricultural development in the Common Market;

2. the achievement of the optimum utilization of agricultural resources; and

3. the improvement of the efficiency of agricultural production in order to increase the supply of agricultural products for

   a. domestic consumption,

   b. exports to regional and extraregional markets, and

   c. inputs for agro-based industries.

Similar to the RIP, a set of activities were identified for regional production utilizing regional resources. Feasibility studies identified the following activities for increased production: grains, legumes, fruits and vegetables, spices and essential oils, livestock and livestock products, fish and fish products, oils and fats. However, there has been no progress on CARICOM's Program for Regional Agricultural Development (CPAD).

## 6.1c  An Assessment of Production Integration Efforts in CARICOM

Generally, CARICOM has had a poor record in its efforts at state-sponsored production integration in industry and agriculture. The failure of these initiatives is directly related to the import-substitution industrialization strategy and the high level of state involvement in managing the development of new activities. A superior policy stance would have been to focus on developing a sustainable set of macroeconomic policies aimed at encouraging private investment in export and import-competing activities. This would have involved removing the hindrances or obstacles affecting intraregional investing flows and factor movements.

The absence of a market-oriented approach to production integration is essentially what was wrong with CARICOM's efforts in this area. Given the greater emphasis *all* CARICOM countries are now placing on the development of exports and the overall shift to an export-oriented development strategy by CARICOM countries, it is now appropriate to refocus CARICOM's efforts and emphasize a market-oriented strategy of production integration. In this approach government would concentrate on providing efficient infrastructure (and administration), the appropriate macroeconomic environment, incentives, and selected support services to assist the private sector. Attempts at determining the location of industry and identifying the set of industries to be developed will no longer be the centerpiece of efforts at production integration. The emphasis would now be on adopting "market friendly" policies, while simultaneously implementing selective policy interventions to compensate for market failure (e.g., export marketing).

Given these considerations there should be a movement away from the state-managed programming approach to regional agricultural and industrial development and toward a more passive role for the state. In the market-oriented approach, the focus would be on adopting and implementing regional agricultural and industrial policy stances that are market-oriented. The state would carefully put in place the appropriate policy regime to stimulate private sector activity in the agricultural and industrial sectors. To encourage private sector activity, vital institutional support services would be provided by the state to overcome the imperfection of the market. Therefore, the state would be facilitating the functioning of the market system, not distorting it, resulting in greater inefficiency.

## 6.1d  The Integration Model and Export Promotion

Contrary to popular belief, the early writers on Caribbean economic integration [Brewster and Thomas (1967); McIntyre (1966)] never envisaged regional integration as an inward-oriented development model. Regional import substitution was an integral part of the integration model, but was seen as complementary to a diversified range of extraregional exports. Worrell (1994) argued that the emphasis that has been placed on the regional harmonization of fiscal incentives was largely in recognition of the importance of foreign investment in stimulating production for exports.

The integration model did identify an important role for exports, but the model was not a regional export-oriented development strategy. The integration model focused on production and the development of new products. It did not specify the range of policies and set of institutional arrangements that would have to be in place to encourage production for the extraregional market relative to the regional market. In other words, the macro and micro policy reforms at the national level that would be necessary to counteract the bias against extraregional exports was not part of the integration model. The assumption appears to have been that once production is increased exports to the extraregional market would also expand. The importance of a regional strategy of export promotion did not influence the architecture of the integration model. In hindsight that was a major failing of development economics in the 1960s in general, and by researchers in particular, on trade and development policy. Intellectual work was still strongly in favor of an import substitution industrialization strategy (ISI) for development countries and little or no work was devoted to the importance of export promotion policies. The failure of the ISI strategy, in particular in Latin America, and the relative success of the export promotion strategy in Asia, has led to strong intellectual support in the 1980s for an outward-oriented development strategy in developing countries.[1] The absence of an explicit policy of export promotion in the original integration model is further illustrated by the role identified for the common external tariff (CET). The CET was originally established to provide a common protective barrier for regional industries to ensure that they satisfied regional demand. Protection was thought to be necessary for learning to occur or to allow producers sufficient time to learn the tricks of the trade to becoming efficient. In other words, the traditional "infant industry" argument was an important theoretical justification for the CET. There was no notion of time-phased protection that would be progressively reduced after the initial learning period had elapsed. In fact, the debate that followed the signing of the Treaty of Chaguaramas has been more focused on achieving regional consensus on the CET and an appropriate implementation period. It is only recently that the conceptual underpinnings of the tariff have been intensely debated.

The implementation of IMF/World Bank structural adjustment programs (SAPs) in the region has precipitated a process of economic liberalization, including trade liberalization. In addition, there has been a global trend toward increased trade liberalization as countries attempt to increase efficiency, improve international competitiveness and expand world trade. These considerations prompted a rethinking of the conceptual basis of the tariff and the promotion of internationally competitive production was identified as the primary objective of the tariff. On the basis of this the heads of government agreed to progressively reduce the CET from 0–5% to 40% in 1993 to 0–5% to 20% in 1998. This represents a fundamental departure from the principles and objectives of the CET that were included in the original integration model.

## 6.2 THE CARICOM SINGLE MARKET AND ECONOMY

Fundamental changes that took place in the world in the latter half of the 1980s include the Single European Market, the Canada-U.S.A. Free Trade Agreement, the North American Free Trade Area, the trend toward globalization of production, the development of a "new" regionalism, the emergence of the Pacific Rim as a center of economic power, and the dismantling of the Soviet bloc. All of these changes have prompted a serious evaluation of the integration strategy and whether it was appropriate to meet the demands of the "new world order." As a result of these factors the CARICOM heads of government in the Grand Anse Declaration of 1989 called for a set of things to be put in place toward the creation of a CARICOM single market and economy (CSME). This marked the adoption of a new integration model and the beginning of the modern phase of the integration movement.

### 6.2a  Defining the CSME

The proposals for a CSME have been structured to build on what is already in place for CARICOM. The CSME will differ from CARICOM only in detail. The Caribbean Common Market's primary, if not exclusive, goal was the achievement of an integrated market via regional trade liberalization. The CSME embraces the concept of market integration, but also emphasizes factor market integration and macroeconomic policy coordination and harmonization. Factor market integration relates to the free movement of labor and capital so as to provide a regional pool of capital and labor to facilitate the regional integration of production. In short, the unrestricted movement of goods, services, capital, and labor defines a common economic space for microeconomic decisions. Supporting macroeconomic policies must be put in place to sustain the common economic space.[2]

The CSME has the following attributes:

a. Free movement of goods and services

b. Factor market integration, that is, the free movement of capital and labor

c. Monetary union

d. Harmonization and coordination of other supporting macroeconomic policies

e. Common external trade policy

The measures that have been identified for the CSME differ somewhat from those that are recommended for a genuine single market and economy.[3] First, not *all* standards would need to be harmonized, but rather a system of a mix of mandatory and voluntary would be implemented. Second, the free circulation of goods was not being contemplated. Third, the free movement of labor does not include the harmonization of social services. Fourth, a single currency would require levels of monetary cooperation that are beyond the present goals of CARICOM, and further study would be required to arrive at a policy.[4] Finally, the achievement of a common external tariff was affected by the presence of differential internal taxes (e.g., consumption tax). Therefore, it should be recognized that the achievement of a "truly" common external tariff would be greater if there was increased harmonization of internal taxes.

In summary, the CSME has the attributes identified in a through e in the list above, but there are some differences in detail from a genuine single market and economy, notably in the area of monetary cooperation.

### 6.2b  The CSME and Export Promotion

Contrary to popular opinion the CSME is not an inward-looking policy, but rather it sees the development of exports, particularly extraregional exports, as the engine of growth in CARICOM. The aim of the CSME policy is to create a single economic space in which regional firms utilizing regional pools of capital and labor can develop and expand viable export- and import-competing industries. The regional market will serve as a stepping-stone to penetrating the "tougher" international markets.

Regional producers will not be provided with highly protective tariffs and QRs to insulate them from international competition. Therefore, there will be strong antiexport bias built in to the regional trade regime to discourage exports. The 1992 heads of government decision to progressively reduce the common external tariff (CET), from 0–5% to 40% in 1990 to 0–5% to 20% by 1998, is designed to increase the international competition faced by regional producers to induce gains in efficiency and improvements in international competitiveness. Unfortunately this has been undermined by the adjustments in indirect taxes that were implemented to compensate for the revenue loses resulting from the tariff reductions.[5] In particular, the adjustments in consumption taxes have probably maintained or increased the nominal level of protection after the first round of CET reductions (see Appendix 1 for the timetable of CET reductions).

Countries that have implemented official IMF/World Bank structural adjustment programs (SAPs) have trade liberalization programs in place and would not have made tax adjustments that would undermine the trade liberalization program. In addition, all of these countries (Jamaica, Guyana, and Trinidad and Tobago) have adopted market-based exchange rates that are expected to adjust to correct for bias in the structure of economic incentives, particularly counteracting antiexport bias.

To support CARICOM countries efforts at export promotion, the CARICOM Export Development Project (CEDP) was established in the 1980s. It has a mandate to provide support systems for regional exporters of manufacturing and agricultural goods. CEDP has provided trade information, marketing assistance, and other areas of technical assistance to exporters, but it has not been allocated adequate resources to support a vibrant regional export thrust.

In summary, the CSME is consistent with a regional strategy of export promotion and the recent regional trade policy reforms are aimed at promoting exports. However, there needs to be a clear articulation of a strategy for regional cooperation in export promotion, and this should be incorporated in the policy timetable for the CSME.

## 6.2c  The CSME and National Structural Adjustment Programs (SAPs)

Regional efforts at achieving a CSME are proceeding at the same time that some CARICOM countries are implementing official IMF/World Bank SAPs. The obvious issue that emerges is whether official SAPs will facilitate or hinder regional effort at achieving a CSME. In addition, does a strategy of economic integration enhance the prospects for a successful structural adjustment program?

SAPs can affect regional economic integration through a variety of channels. SAPs emphasize the removal of policy interventions and regulatory controls in the market system. The liberalization of factor markets should facilitate the free movement of labor and capital, which is an important objective of the CSME.

Regulatory reforms that remove legal and institutional barriers to the free movement of goods and services expand the possibilities for increased intraregional trade and investment. In short, SAPs emphasize market liberalization, which, if appropriately designed, can facilitate the market integration targeted by the CSME.

Conceptually, SAPs can and should promote regional economic integration by facilitating market integration. However, in practice IMF/World Bank

SAPs in most cases have tended to exacerbate unstable macroeconomic conditions in developing countries, resulting in the persistence of weak growth, high unemployment, shortages of foreign exchange, and high levels of external indebtedness. Macroeconomic instability, together with weak economic performance, undermine any country's efforts at promoting regional economic integration. Therefore, SAPs can begin to assist CARICOM countries in their efforts at regional economic integration by achieving a higher level of macroeconomic stability and improved overall economic performance. If these conditions are achieved, there will be less practical difficulty in achieving the CSME.[6]

Economic integration can also improve the prospects for successful structural adjustment in CARICOM economies. In other words, significant progress toward the achievement of a CSME can increase the likelihood of successful structural adjustment. This can be done by increasing (and improving) regional policy coordination at the macro and micro levels. Important objectives of the SAPs in CARICOM are higher growth, export diversification, and adequate levels of foreign exchange.

The West Indian Commission and the CARICOM Council of Central Bank Governors have argued that fiscal discipline is a necessary condition for a stable exchange rate and improving the balance of payments position of CARICOM countries. In both cases it was argued that fiscal discipline was most likely to be achieved through the instrumentality of a CARICOM Monetary Authority, which had clear and strict rules relating to deficit financing.[7] Researchers have shown that fiscal behavior is very influential in determining the exchange rate, inflation rate, and nominal interest rates [see Worrell (1987), Bourne et al. (1985); and St. Cyr (1981)]. To the extent that there is a strong relationship between these variables, regional integration would assist in facilitating the goals of SAPs, notably growth and exchange rate stability.

The CSME through the achievement of market integration would allow CARICOM enterprises to merge, if necessary, to become internationally competitive. This would result in greater efficiency and higher product quality. The globalization of production is encouraging the growth of strategic alliances among different firms across national boundaries. This allows firms to maximize comparative advantage and results in greater specialization in production. CARICOM enterprises should be encouraged to become regional entities and participate in the process of globalization to improve their efficiency and overall competitiveness.

Economic integration could also result in resource policy and information sharing in technology transfer, research and development, and export promotion and marketing. Increased economic cooperation at the regional level to assist national export promotion efforts would be an important channel through which regional integration could facilitate successful SAPs in CARICOM.

In summary, regional efforts at achieving a CSME can facilitate the implementation of successful SAPs in CARICOM. The difficulties that arise are more related to the design and sequencing of some policies in SAPs under the guidance of the IMF and the World Bank. But conceptually there is no inconsistency between economic integration and successful SAPs. In fact, SAPs can also assist in achieving integration objectives by removing policy interventions, regulations, and legal barriers to the integration of markets for goods, services, and factors (specifically capital and labor). In addition, regional cooperation in export promotion can assist countries pursuing export-oriented medium-term adjustment strategies at the national level.

## 6.3 REGIONAL INTEGRATION: THE WAY FORWARD

### 6.3a Implementation Is the Achilles' Heel

Despite the fact that CARICOM governments have stated their intentions to achieve a CSME, very little progress has been made. In fact, CARICOM does not have a good record of regional policy implementation since the signing of the Treaty of Chaguaramas in 1974. The West Indies Commission (WIC) Report[8] identified CARICOM's poor implementation record as the major constraint to the process of regional integration. In commenting on the problem of regional policy implementation the WIC Report summed up the problem as follows:

If the integration movement is to be strengthened, if it is to recover lost ground and respond to the demands of the present and the future, the West Indies must put in place machinery that overcomes this weakness. The weakness itself should not surprise us; it is not that the regional machinery for implementation has broken down or is otherwise inadequate to its task; it is simply non-existent. It was never put in place. Perhaps in the beginning, that was a tolerable omission. Such decisions as needed implementation could be left to action in national capitals. However, the experience of 25 years since Dickenson Bay, and more particularly of 19 years since Chaguaramas has demonstrated beyond serious argument that regional integration requires regional machinery endowed with the capacity to make integration effective. (WIC Report, 1992: 463)

The WIC suggested that a CARICOM commission be established to deal with the problem of policy implementation using people with vast regional experience (e.g., ex-prime ministers). The heads of government, in reviewing the recommendations of the WIC, accepted that there was a problem of implementation but rejected the proposal for a CARICOM commission. Instead, a Bureau of heads of government comprising the past chairman of CARICOM, the existing chairman, and the future chairman was agreed upon as the most effective institutional arrangement for improving regional policy implementation. It is too early to judge the effectiveness or lack of effectiveness of the bureau. Suffice it to say that the bureau has not been able to further the implementation of policies aimed at achieving a CSME. It would appear that the problem of regional policy implementation is still the Achilles' heel of the regional integration movement. The problem will have to be seriously reviewed again and a more effective solution arrived at. Failure to do so will probably result in increased disillusionment with CARICOM resulting in the increased fragmentation of the region. Given the fundamental changes taking place in the global economy, including the resurgence of regionalism, this is an outcome that must be prevented.

### 6.3b  The Way Forward

If the problem of implementation can be overcome, one could suggest that the integration movement focus on four key policy areas:

a. Export promotion

b. Macroeconomic policy coordination (particularly Monetary Union)

c. Factor market integration, that is, the free movement of capital and labor (particularly skilled labor)

d. External economic relations

In the earlier discussion items a, b, and c have been discussed. It should be noted that all CARICOM countries are now pursuing export-oriented development strategies. There is a lot of potential for economies of scale and scope if there is regional cooperation in efforts at export promotion. The CARICOM Export Development Agency (CEDP) provides important services to regional exporters, particularly in the areas of trade information, and marketing and promotion. CEDP must be strengthened and developed to assist service (other than in tourism) exporters (e.g., information processing, desktop publishing, telemarketing, and architectural design). Regional cooperation in the area of investment promotion is absolutely essential. Competing against each other for private investment into the region is not productive for the region as a whole. If the barriers to intraregional investment are removed, the region can then be promoted as a single unit rather than individual territories.

The emergence of large trading blocs (e.g., NAFTA) and the associated rise in "regionalism" in developing countries has heightened the importance of external economic relations to the development prospects of CARICOM. Negotiating international economic arrangements to complement and, in some cases, replace the existing agreements will be a major policy objective of CARICOM in the medium/long-term.

Rapid technological change that has lead to the globalization of production, which essentially means the spatial location of the products process in separate geographical areas to take advantage of differences in comparative advantage across countries, has fueled the growth of regional integration movements. The globalization process has forced countries to widen their economic space beyond national boundaries, and this is not likely to be a temporary phenomenon. As part of this process Venezuela has concluded a Free Trade Agreement with CARICOM, and Columbia is in the process of negotiating a trade and economic cooperation agreement. CARICOM is going to have to become far more proactive in deepening its economic relationships with developed and developing countries with whom it can expand trade and increase investment. This is going to be an essential plank of regional economic policy as the region attempts to expand and diversify its exports and increase the flows of private investment. Up to this point CARICOM has only reacted to initiatives of other countries for a deeper economic relationship. In the "new world order" the region will need to be active in pursuing its economic interests beyond national and regional boundaries.

In conclusion, economic integration has always been an important plank of trade and development policy in CARICOM countries. The early writers on economic integration focused on the integration of goods markets and the trade-related benefits of integration. In addition, the integration of production was seen as a state-managed process implemented through programing schemes. The recent approach to integration emphasizes the benefits that are derived from macroeconomic policy coordination and harmonization. The pursuit of a CARICOM Single Market and Economy has been influenced by the recent insights about the "time" benefits of integration.

In response to problems of low growth, high unemployment, chronic shortages of foreign exchange, and unsustainable levels of external debt, some CARICOM countries have been forced to implement official structural adjustment programs (SAPs) with the IMF and the World Bank. The SAPs can have an important influence on efforts at regional integration and the latter can also facilitate successful SAPs.

Given these considerations and the fundamental changes taking place in the world economy, the integration movement should emphasize the following policy areas: export promotion, macroeconomic policy coordination and harmonization, factor market integration, and external economic relations. Given the emergence of large trading blocs and the growth in regionalism, CARICOM countries need to put in place a set of external arrangements that facilitates the growth of exports and increases the levels of investment. This would be entirely consistent with the export oriented development strategies that all of the countries have indicated they wish to pursue in the medium/long term.

## NOTES

1. See Bhagwati (1988) for a useful review of the early debate in the 1950s and 1960s on export promotion vis-à-vis import substitution. Bhagwati refers to the overwhelming intellectual influence of the "export pessimists" in this period.

2. The recent literature on economic integration [see de Melo and Panagariya (1992); and Robson (1993)] has placed greater emphasis on the economic benefits to be derived from macroeconomic policy coordination and harmonization. The economic benefits to be derived from policy coordination or policy harmonization center around gains in economic efficiency. Policy coordination or harmonization by reducing transactions, costs, and eliminating policy barriers to resource mobility within the single market and the economy should result in greater efficiency in resource allocation.

3. See CARICOM (1991: xi).

4. Since the Grand Anse Declaration in 1989 a Council of Central Bank Governors of all CARICOM countries has been formed and they have analyzed the issue of a single currency very carefully. Specific proposals for the achievements of a single currency were made by the Council of Central Bank Governors. However, as a result of the floating of the Trinidad and Tobago dollar in 1993 the heads of government decided to review the whole issue of a single market again.

5. Worrell (1987) estimates that import-competing production is approximately 5% or less in CARICOM countries and there is no real choice between producing for the export and domestic market. The low level of import substitution is largely a result of the small size of the domestic market in the individual countries. There are no strong similarities to the inward-looking trade regimes in Latin America in the 1970s and 1980s with large, monopolistic import-substituting industries producing almost exclusively for the domestic market. Note that exports to the regional market is hard currency (U.S. dollar) trade and cannot really be distinguished from extraregional exports and thus no distinction is made between regional and extraregional exports.

6. Macro stability and improved economic performance are not necessary and sufficient conditions for the achievement of the CSME. Perhaps the most influential factor is political commitment on the part of *all* member states.

7. The experience of the OECS countries with monetary union and a single monetary authority (the Eastern Caribbean Central Bank) greatly influenced the policy position adopted by the West Indian Commission and the Council of Central Bank Governors.

8. In 1989 the Grand Anse Declaration of the CARICOM heads of government proposed that a West Indian Commission be established to help the people of the West Indies prepare for the twenty-first century. The Commission had the following mandate:

   a. the commission should be an independent body;

   b. the commission should report to heads of government prior to their meeting in July 1992;

   c. the commission should formulate proposals for advancing the goals of the Treaty of Chaguaramas which established the Caribbean community and Common Market (CARICOM) in 1973.

# 7

## Future Directions for Research

The results of the analyses in this book provide motivation for further investigation into specific areas of the CARICOM countries export performance. Specifically, the institutional analysis and modeling could be carried out at a more micro level. This is particularly interesting since there are distinct policy implications to be drawn from the results of these analyses. In this chapter some of the major areas for future work in both the institutional analysis and modeling of the export performance are discussed.

### 7.1 MODELING THE EXPORT SECTOR

In doing this research I was amazed at the absence of empirical research at the micro level on the export sector.[1] Studies using firm-specific—level or industry—data to test alternative propositions or review export performance were virtually nonexistent. Ayub's (1981) study of the Jamaican manufacturing sector and two doctoral theses—Farrell (1979) and Downes (1985)—looking at the performance and development contribution of the manufacturing sectors in Trinidad and Tobago and Barbados were the only micro studies that were available. One should note that none of these studies focused specifically on exports although there was discussion of issues related to export performance.

It is not inconceivable that the dearth of micro empirical studies of the export sector might be due to the absence of data at the industry or firm levels. The major CARICOM countries—Jamaica, Barbados, and Trinidad and Tobago[2]—do annual surveys of industrial establishments, but the data derived are too aggregative and descriptive (e.g., number of firms per industry).

There is an urgent need for periodic detailed industrial surveys that try to measure capital stocks across industries, as well as to provide information on technology acquisition, skill distribution of workers, export orders, monthly employment patterns, to mention a few areas. Related to this is the need for input/output tables for these economies. The collection of data for the preparation of input/output matrices has to be institutionalized in statistical departments.

One of the reasons for applying export supply models mainly to nontraditional exports was that total aggregate exports are far too aggregative. Although the results of modeling nontraditional exports are instructive, it can be argued that models focusing on a country's key individual nontraditional exports would be of greater value and, as mentioned earlier, would certainly improve export policy formulation. But to estimate industry-specific models requires industry-specific data as referred to above.

In terms of policy implications an important factor in modeling export behavior is to capture the influence of "incentives" on export flows. In this context the microbased measure of the effective exchange rate, which includes the effect of both the restrictiveness of the import regime and the degree of export subsidization, is preferable to the more macro real effective exchange rate that measures the relative price of tradables. The former is preferable principally because it captures the competition between EP and IS activities. Worrell (1987) argues that given the low level of IS activity, the issue in CARICOM countries is not the competition between EP and IS activities but rather tradable (mainly EP) versus nontradable. The more aggregative real effective exchange rate, although not as useful, provides vital information on the incentive structure. Therefore, policy formulation requires information on both the relative price of tradable to nontradables as well as within the former category, the relative profitability of exports.

The computation of the effective exchange rate measuring the relative profitability of exports will necessitate the compilation of time series data on export incentives—subsidies, preferential loans, and so on, and import restrictions—tariff rates, rebates, drawbacks, quantitative restrictions, and the like. This is a time-consuming research task and will require the close collaboration of a number of government agencies.

An interesting feature of CARICOM export development is the growing importance of service exports other than tourism. Although data are very patchy and nontourist service exports are presently not major earners of foreign exchange, most public officials suggest that they may be the major export industry of the future.[3] In the collection of firm- and industry-level data and the documentation of incentives, one must remember to include the nontourism service industries.

## 7.2  INSTITUTIONAL ANALYSIS

The collection of time series data on the set of export incentives and the restrictions on the import regime will necessitate a comprehensive documentation of export incentives.[4] What is of particular importance is some quantitative feel for the impact of individual incentives on exporters. Furthermore, one needs to know in what areas exporters believe incentives are needed most.

Complementary to the modeling exercises should be surveys of exporting firms that try to distill the information on the effectiveness of export incentives. Once again the results would enhance export policy formulation and permit a continuous evaluation of the incentive system. A study sponsored by the World Bank [see Rhee, Ross-Larson, and Russell (1984)] is a useful guide to the type of survey envisaged.

Our analysis in Chapter 3 tells us that price-related incentives are not the only elements to consider in encouraging exports. The nonprice aspects of export promotion are as important in any thrust toward export promotion. It is also suggested that research done at the World Bank had pointed to the importance of institutional support to exports, particularly in the area of export marketing.[5] It is absolutely vital that information is gathered on how CARICOM exporters penetrate extraregional markets. Is it through first buyers as in the east Asian case or through individual promotional efforts? In the area of nontraditional exports, specifically manufactured exports, the subsector appears to be dualistic in character in CARICOM. It is split between a largely foreign-owned export-oriented group of firms[6] selling mainly to the U.S. market and locally owned firms focusing on the protected CARICOM market. These differences should be built in to the analysis. An important factor is to get the response of locally owned firms or joint ventures that sell some proportion of their output on the extraregional market. It is also important to analyze the set of factors (or incentives) that could induce local firms focusing on the CARICOM market to begin to export to the extraregional market. One suspects that effective assistance in the area of export marketing might be useful here.

One should also consider specifically the "new" service exports in looking at issues related to nonprice incentives. In the area of export markets a similar set of questions could be focused on firms operating in the "new" service areas. Given its infancy export consultancy advice of the type discussed in Chapter 3 in reference to manufacturing firms could be of vital importance to firms in the "new" service industries. Therefore, it is important for research to provide some insight into the areas where assistance is most needed and will be the most effective in expanding export sales.

A related aspect of the institutional analysis that is necessary and, once again, has policy significance, is the identification of the bottlenecks and delays in the governments' bureaucracy that adversely affects exporters.[7]

One of the strengths of the outward-oriented development strategies adopted by the east Asian NIEs is the efficiency of public institutions in a wide range of areas, including port handling, processing of foreign investment applications, granting of import duty waivers, payment of claims for import duties, processing of applications for short-term working capital financing, and the processing of applications to the EPZs [see Bhattacharya and Linn (1988); Amsden (1989)].

Statements from private sector manufacturers associations and discussions with individual firms cite lengthy administrative delays as a constant constraint to speedy responses for export orders. Manufacturers suggest that implementing increased efficiency at the port, particularly in Barbados, demands urgent attention. Generally, there needs to be a study for each country that comprehensively documents the range of administrative bottlenecks that adversely affect exports. At a recent conference sponsored by the Barbados Export Promotion Corporation on export promotion, officials and private entrepreneurs from Korea, Hong Kong, Mauritius, and Kenya pointed to the importance of removing administrative delays in developing effective institutional support for exports.

In conclusion, the results of the research raise some potentially interesting research questions in specific areas related to the development of nontraditional exports in CARICOM countries. It is not possible to answer all of the questions in a single work, but the issues that arose in doing the research are worthy of discussion.

Essentially, more microresearch is required in economic modeling and institutional analysis of the export performance. A critical constraint to microempirical studies is the weak data base that exists. In the absence of improvement in the official statistics, researchers need to carry out surveys of the export manufacturing sector and "new" services sector to derive firm-level and industry-specific data for empirical work. There are substantial benefits to export policy formulation from detailed microempirical studies. There is a lot of diversity in the response to various export incentives across industries and these studies should provide useful insights into these issues.

The research points out that export performance is largely influenced by supply considerations. In this context the impact of "incentives" on export performance is an important issue but far from the only one. The modeling attempts can be enhanced by the compilation of time series data on export subsidies and so on that permits the computation of the more microeffective exchange rate that measures the relative profitability of exports. Complementary to this is the need for research on the administration of export incentives and the bottlenecks or delays that are encountered by exporters.

## NOTES

1. The dearth of research was an additional motivation for this book.

2. Guyana is also a major CARICOM country but it does not carry out annual surveys of industrial establishments.

3. This was revealed during discussions with officials at the Export Promotion Organizations in Jamaica and Barbados. In the former case the reference is really to offshore information services—data processing and telemarketing—and in the latter case to offshore information services and offshore banking and insurance.

4. This exercise in itself is useful since there are incentives that have been legislated that exporters are completely unaware of. Thus this would serve to broaden exporters information base.

5. I devised a questionnaire (based on a section of the survey done in 1984 by Rhee, Ross-Larson, and Russell, of Korea) on export marketing. The response rate in Barbados was extremely poor and I canceled it when increased responses were not forthcoming.

6. A lot of these are firms operating in the industrial estates or EPZs and in many cases are taking advantage of the U.S. 807 program.

7. The research suggestion is prompted by the discussions I held with some firms in Jamaica, Trinidad and Tobago, and Barbados. One must note that I am also including port and airport services here.

# 8

## Conclusion

In the introduction two basic objectives were set: First, to define the role of exports in the small, open CARICOM economies; Second, given the importance of exports to these economies, to determine the major factors responsible for the weak export performance observed in the last twenty years. In this last chapter the main points made in this book are briefly summarized and the more important conclusions obtained are presented.

Caribbean economists have always pointed out the importance of exports to the process of economic growth and development in these economies. From the early writings of Lewis (1950) through to the institutional analysis of the dependency or "Plantation school" models of Best and Levitt (1968) and Beckford (1972) to the more recent work of Worrell (1987; 1989), the role of exports in economic development has always been stressed.

In the development economics literature a body of empirical work has pointed to the strong positive correlation between exports and GDP growth. The traditional approach is a simple production function framework, with the primary factors (labor and capital) and exports as arguments in the function. The results showed a positive correlation between exports and GDP growth over a wide range of developing countries and a variety of time periods. Anecdotal evidence pointed to the special importance of exports. A variety of arguments were advanced relating to economies of scale, increased efficiency due to international competition, and technological change to mention a few.

Feder (1983) argues that all of these arguments point to higher marginal factor productivities in the export sector than in the nonexport sector. Feder builds a two-sector model that allows us to test for differential factor productivities using aggregate data. The model also emphasizes the dynamic growth effects or "externalities" of exports on the nonexport sector. Despite the fact that small developing countries tend to be more open to international trade, the empirical research has not previously focused on the role of exports in small country growth (including the CARICOM countries).

Chapter 4 empirically estimates Feder's model for a sample of twenty-two small developing countries (including fourteen middle-income countries) over the period 1965–1989, and twenty-five small developing countries (including sixteen middle income countries) over the subperiods 1965–1980 and 1980–1989. The main purpose here is to test the "externality" argument about the role of exports in small country growth. The results do not provide strong support for the externality argument but there is some support for the hypothesis among the eighteen small middle income developing countries over both sample periods.

More recent research [see Esfahani (1991)] points out that Feder-type models neglect the importance of the foreign exchange contribution of exports in reducing import "shortages" thereby enhancing growth. In other words, the "externality" argument is not the only proposition relating to the role of exports in small developing countries.

In Chapter 4 it is argued that the foreign exchange contribution of exports is their most important role in Caribbean-type economies. It is argued that the productive sectors are heavily dependent on a wide range of imports of intermediate and capital goods. Therefore, output expansion necessitates increased foreign exchange flows to finance the needed imports. It is suggested that in CARICOM economies import dependence is such that foreign flows are important for production even in the absence of import "shortages" or import rationing. In addition, it is argued that all sources of foreign exchange flows—exports of goods and services, foreign grants, loans, capital inflows—are important. However, exports can be distinguished for they have certain other positive developmental contributions relating to employment, technological change, balance of payments improvement, and so on.

A simple model is built to test the proposition of the importance of foreign exchange flows to output. Using a Cobb-Douglas production framework, imports enter as an argument in the production function. An equation is specified for imports that is substituted into the production function and the resulting equation is estimated. The model explains a large proportion of the variation in the dependent variable (real GDP), and foreign exchange flows are statistically significant. The results do provide support for the foreign exchange contribution of exports hypothesis.

Given the importance of exports to CARICOM economies, the weak export performance that has been observed in the last twenty years must be a source of great concern. Providing a detailed description of the export performance highlighting the major areas of concern, is a necessary condition for far more technical analysis of the export performance.

In Chapter 2 conventional techniques (nonstochastic) of descriptive analysis are employed to describe the export performance of CARICOM's major economies—Barbados, Jamaica, and Trinidad and Tobago—in the 1970–1988 period.

The tools used are the constant market share (CMS) analysis of the total export and manufactured export performance and the revealed comparative advantage (RCA) indexes. The results indicate that the export performance in the 1970–1987 period has not been impressive, particularly in Jamaica. However, one should note that the performance of the tourist industry in Barbados and Jamaica generally was encouraging. The manufactured export performance was invariably good in the 1970–1979 subperiod but deteriorated sharply in the 1979–1988 subperiod. The results suggest that for both total exports and manufactured exports supply-side considerations were important factors in these countries export performance.

Consistent with the CMS and RCA results the focus of the more detailed analysis of the export performance was on the supply side. Two approaches were adopted in analyzing the export performance of CARICOM countries: First, because it is strongly argued in the literature, based on the successful experience of the east Asian NIEs, that reducing or removing antiexport bias and creating neutral incentives to EP and IS activities are a necessary conditions for the growth of exports. (In Chapter 3 an attempt is made to look at the issue of antiexport bias in CARICOM economies via real effective exchange rates). The removal of antiexport bias is achieved via tariff reform and the introduction of export development policies. In the literature, notably from the World Bank, a set of export policy instruments are recommended for developing countries based on the experience of the east Asian NIEs. Against this background the set of export incentives adopted by the major CARICOM countries is analyzed. It is found that weaknesses in the export policy instruments adopted by these countries have constrained the development of nontraditional exports contributing to the weak export performance that is observed.

In Chapter 3 the major instruments of export development in the east Asian experience are listed:

1. Realistic exchange rates

2. Free input and output trade

3. Ready access to export finance

4. Access to primary and nontraded inputs to undistorted prices

5. Adequate institutional infrastructure for trade

6. Free trade zones

The above set of export policy instruments are suggested to developing countries as export development policies to complement the reform of the protective system aimed at removing antiexport bias and stimulating export growth.

The behavior of the real effective exchange rates in the 1968–1988 period provides some tentative evidence of antiexport bias in Trinidad and Tobago and Barbados. In Jamaica the REER depreciated continuously after 1977, indicating an increase in the relative price of tradables. Given the low level of production for the domestic market this should have positively affected exports. However, our description of the export performance in Chapter 2 pointed to a weak performance in Jamaica particularly in the case of manufactured exports. This is tentative evidence that "incentives" were not stimulating a strong export response. A lot of variations in the REER is observed in Jamaica indicating that the structure of incentives was unstable over time and thus not favorable to encouraging increased levels of private investment. Therefore creating improved "incentives" and removing antiexport bias is important but probably more important is achieving stable incentives and a sustainable policy regime.

CARICOM countries adopted a range of export policy instruments to reduce antiexport bias and stimulate exports particularly nontraditional exports. Export development policies were described under the following headings:

1. Fiscal incentives

2. The role of the exchange rate

3. Export processing zone's (EPZs)

4. Trade financing

5. Institutional support for exporters: export promotion organizations

The analysis in Chapter 3 points to the fact that in the east Asian economies, after the adoption of an export promotion strategy, a range of price and nonprice incentives were adopted to support exports and maintain them over a long period of time. In contrast, in CARICOM economies export policies have been adopted in a piecemeal fashion with no concerted policy effort to encourage exports over a long period of time. The weaknesses in export development policy have adversely affected the growth of nontraditional exports. There is an urgent need for policy reform and the policy lesson drawn from the east Asian NIEs suggests new policy directions in fiscal incentives, trade financing, assistance from EPOs and the role of EPZs. Exchange rate adjustments or any individual policy changes will not improve the export performance. It is going to require changes in a range of price and nonprice areas to create the environment to foster export development.

In Chapter 5 the influence of "incentives" on export flows is captured by the real effective exchange rate. The real effective exchange rate is assumed to be an exogenous variable that can be adjusted by policy. In fact, any policy that shifts the relative price of tradables, exchange rate adjustment, wage rates, and so forth, will affect the real effective exchange rate. In the computation of the real effective exchange rate, different weighting schemes have been adopted to test whether the results are sensitive to different weights. In addition, the choice of weights gives the real effective exchange rate a different interpretation providing useful policy insights.

The empirical results indicate that "incentives" have a significant influence on export flows and the elasticity of supply in some cases is greater than 1. Furthermore, the results are sensitive to different weighting schemes. The real effective exchange rate based on the aggregate export weights of the country's major trading partners consistently performs better than any of the other measures. This measure of the real effective exchange rate assumes that domestic producers in the importing country are the major sources of competition for the country's exporters.

The econometric evidence highlights the importance of incentives to export performance. These results are complementary to the earlier institutional analysis in Chapter 3 and further support the case for policy reform to improve the effectiveness of export incentives. It would be incorrect to interpret these results as a case for competitive devaluations in CARICOM economies. One should note that the relative price of tradables can be adjusted by other means than the exchange rate (e.g., via wage restraint or an incomes policy).

In Chapter 6 the regional dimension of trade and development policy in CARICOM is considered. Regional integration has always been an important plank of development policy in CARICOM countries and market integration has been viewed as critical to stimulating increases in output, investment, and exports. The principal problem has been the lack of implementation of economic policy agreed to at the regional level by national governments. To complement and improve the effectiveness of national export-oriented development strategies there must be a vibrant economic integration movement. The unrestricted movement of goods, services, and other actors (notably capital and skilled labor) is a necessary condition for increasing the investment opportunities and possibilities for export diversification in the region. Therefore, in the contemporary situation the achievement of a CARICOM single market and economy must be seen as a vital component of national export-oriented development strategies or official structural adjustment programs that are centered around an export-oriented policy regime.

Although some important conclusions are drawn from the study, research points to specific areas worthy of further intense investigation. The most obvious research area is the need for microempirical studies of the performance of individual nontraditional exports. The absence of the relevant data is the major constraint and researchers will have to construct their own surveys to generate the data. There are a variety of responses across industries to "incentives," and this can be captured by industry-specific studies. There are significant benefits to be gained for the formulation of export policies.

Finally, as argued earlier, both price and nonprice incentives are important to the development of exports. In this context the identification of the key areas of administrative bottlenecks or delays will help to improve the efficiency of exporters and their overall competitiveness. Research is needed to examine the administration of export incentives and identify the key administrative bottlenecks or delays.

# Works Cited

Adams, F. G., Behrman, J. R., and Boldin, M. (1989), "Productivity, Competitiveness and Export Growth in Developing Countries," mimeo., University of Pennsylvania, Economics Department.

Ali, I., (1979), "India's Manufactured Exports: An Analysis of Supply Factors," *The Developing Economies*, 25, no. 2.

Amsden, A., (1989), *Asia's Next Giant* (Clarendon: Oxford University Press).

Ayub, M., (1981), *Made in Jamaica*, World Bank Staff Occasional Papers #31, (Washington, D.C.: World Bank Publications).

Balassa, B., (1977), "Revealed Comparative Advantage Revisited: An Analysis of Relative Export Shares of the Industrial Countries, 1953–1971," *Manchester School of Economics and Statistics*, 45: 327–44.

Balassa, B., (1985), "Exports, Policy Choices, and Economic Growth in Developing Countries after the 1973 Oil Shock," *Journal of Development Economics* 18, no. 1: 23–25.

Balassa, B., (1965), "Trade Liberalization and 'Revealed Comparative Advantage.' " *The Manchester School of Economics*, 33: 99–124.

Banerji, R., (1974), "The Export Performance of Less Developed Countries: A Constant Market Share Analysis." *Weltwirtschaftliches Archiv*, Band 110, Heft 3: 447–82.

Beckford, G. L., (1972), *Persistent Poverty: Underdevelopment in Plantation Economies of the Third World* (Clarendon: Oxford University Press).

Best, L., and Levitt, K., (1968), "Export Propelled Growth and Industrialization," mimeo, (Montreal: Centre for Developing Area Studies, McGill University.

Bhagwati, J., (1978), *Anatomy and Consequences of Trade Regime's* (Cambridge, Mass.: National Bureau of Economic Research).

Bhagwati, J., (1988), "Export-Promoting Trade Strategy: Issues and Evidence," *World Bank Research Observer* 3, no. 1, January.

Bhattacharya, A., and Linn, J. F., (1988), "Trade and Industrial Policies in the Developing Countries of East Asia," World Bank Discussion Paper no. 28, (Washington, D.C.: World Bank Publications).

Binswanger, H. P., (1974), "A Cost Function Approach to the Measurement of Elasticities of Factor Demand and Elasticities of Substitution," *American Journal of Agricultural Economics* 56: 377–86.

Boamah, D., and Craigwell, R., (1990), "Import Demand in Barbados: A Production Theory Approach," mimeo, Research Department, Central Bank of Barbados.

Bourne, C., Worrell, D., Cor, W., and Solaris, F. (1985), "Exchange Rate Policy Within the CARICOM Community." (CARICOM Secretariat/Inter-American Development Bank, Mimeo).

Brewster, H., and Thomas, C. Y., (1967), *The Dynamics of West Indian Economic Integration* (Jamaica: Institute of Social and Economic Research, University of the West Indies).

CARICOM, (1991), *Towards A CARICOM Single Market and Economy* (Georgetown, Guyana).

Chow, G. C., (1960), "Tests of Equality Between Sets of Coefficients in Two Linear Regressions." *Econometrica* 28: 591–605.

Christensen, L. R., Jorgenson, D. W., Lau, L. J., (1973), "Transcendental Logarithmic Production Frontiers," *Review of Economics and Statistics* 55: 28–45.

Cox, W., and Worrell, D., (1979), "Export Growth and Diversification in the Performance of the Barbadian Economy 1957–77," mimeo, Research Department, Central Bank of Barbados.

Demas, W. G., (1965), *The Economics of Development in Small Countries with Special Reference to the Caribbean* (Canada: McGill University Press).

de Melo, J., and Panagariya, A., (1992), "The New Regionalism in Trade Policy," (Washington: The World Bank and CEPR).

Diewert, E., and Morrison, C., (1986), "Export Supply and Import Demand Functions: A Production Theory Approach," University of British Columbia, Discussion Paper, pp. 86–100.

Donges, J. B. and Riedel, J., (1977), "The Expansion of Manufactured Exports in Developing Countries: An Empirical Assessment of Supply and Demand Issues," *Weltwirtschaftliches Archiv,* Band 113: 58–87.

Downes, A., (1985), "Industrial Growth and Employment in a Small Developing Country: The Case of Barbados 1955–80," doctoral thesis, (Manchester, U.K.: Manchester University).

Erzon, R., Cobb, J., and Holmes, P., (1990), "Effects of the Multi-Fibre Arrangement on Developing Countries' Trade: An Empirical Investigation," in Cable, V., ed., *The Multi-Fibre Arrangement and Developing Countries* (Washington D.C.: World Bank Publications).

Esfahani, H. S., (1991), "Exports, Imports and Economic Growth in Semi-Industrialised Countries," *Journal of Development Economics* 35, no. 1, (January 1991): 93–111.

Faini, R., (1988), "Export Supply, Capacity and Relative Prices," mimeo, Research Department, International Monetary Fund, Washington D.C.

Farrell, T., (1979), "The Structure, Organization and Performance of Manufacturing Industry in Trinidad & Tobago," Ph.D. thesis, University of Toronto.

Farrell, T.M.A., (1982), "Some Short Notes Towards Economic Transformation in the Caribbean," mimeo, Department of Economics, U.W.I., St. Augustine, Trinidad.

Feder, G., (1983), "On Exports and Economic Growth," *Journal of Development Economics*, (February/April): 59–73.

Fosu, A. K., (1990), "Exports and Economic Growth: The African Case," *World Development*, 18, no. 6: 831–35.

Girvan, N., (1972), *Foreign Capital and Economic Underdevelopment in Jamaica*, Institute of Social and Economic Research, University of the West Indies, Mona, Jamaica.

Girvan, N., Samuel, W., Boxhill, I., and Whitehead, J., (1993), *Framework, Areas and Support Measures for Production Integration in CARICOM*, study prepared for the CARICOM Secretariat, August.

Goldstein, M., and Khan, M. S., (1984), "Income and Price Effects in Foreign Trade," in Jones, R. W., and Kenen, P. B., eds., *Handbook of International Economics*, (Amsterdam: North-Holland).

Hemphill, W. L., (1974), "The Effects of Foreign Exchange Receipts on Imports of Less Developed Countries, *IMF Staff Papers* (November): 637–77.

Hilaire, A., (1989), "Economic Reaction to a Sectoral Boom: Trinidad and Tobago 1973–1985," Ph.D. dissertation, Columbia University.

International Monetary Fund, (1970, 1974, 1979, 1984, 1987, and 1991), *Balance of Payments Statistics*, (Washington, D.C.:IMF Publications).

International Monetary Fund, *International Financial Statistics*, (Various Issues).

Jalan, B., (1982), "Classification of Economies by Size," in Jalan, B., ed., *Problems and Policies in Small Economies* (London: Crown Helm, Ltd.).

Jones, R. W., and Kenen, P. B., (1984), *Handbook of International Economics: Volume 1* (Amsterdam: North Holland and Elsevier Science Publishers).

Keesing, D. B., (1988), "Marketing Manufactured Exports from Developing Countries: How to Provide Excellent, Cost-Effective Institutional Support," Trade Policy Division, (Washington, D.C.: World Bank).

Keesing, D. B., and Lall, S., (1988), "Marketing Manufactured Exports from Developing Countries: Information Links, Buyers' Orders and Institutional Support," WIDER mimeo, Helsinki, August.

Khan, M. S., (1974), "Import Demand and Export Demand in Developing Countries," *Staff Papers*, 21, International Monetary Fund, (November): 679–93.

Khan, M. S., and Knight, M.D., (1988), "Import Compression and Export Performance in Developing Countries," *Review of Economics and Statistics* 70, no. 2: 315–22.

Kohli, U. R., (1978), "A Gross National Product Function and the Derived Demand for Imports and Supply of Exports," *Canadian Journal of Economics* 11, no. 12.

Krueger, A., (1978), *Foreign Trade Regimes and Economic Development: Liberalization Attempts and Consequences* (Cambridge, Mass.: Ballinger).

Leamer, E., (1984), *Sources of International Comparative Advantage* (Cambridge: MIT Press).

Leamer, E., and Stern, R., (1970), *Quantitative International Economics* (Cambridge, Mass.: Cambridge University Press).

Lewis, W. A., (1950), "The Industrialization of the British West Indies," *Social and Economic Studies*, Manchester University.

Love, J., (1984), "External Market Conditions, Competitiveness, Diversification and LDC's Exports," *Journal of Development Economics* 16: 279–91.

Limpumba, N., Ndulu. B., Horton, S., and Plourde, A., (1989), "A Supply Constrained Macroeconometric Model of Tanzania," *Economic Modelling*, 5, no. 4.

Maciejewski, E., (1983), " 'Real' " Effective Exchange Rate Indices: A Re-examination of the Major Conceptual and Methodological Issues," *IMF Staff Papers*.

McIntyre, A., (1966), "Some Issues of Trade Policy in the West Indies," *New World Quarterly*, 2, no. 2.

Michaely, M., (1977), "Exports and Growth: An Empirical Investigation," *Journal of Development Economics* 4: 49–53.

Myrdal, G., (1957), *Economic Theory and Underdeveloped Regions* (London: Macmillan).

Nurkse, R., (1961), "Patterns of Trade and Development" in Gottfried Harberler, ed., *Equilibrium and Growth in the World Economy* (Cambridge, Mass.: Cambridge University Press).

Park, J. H., (1991), "Exports and Economic Growth in Developing Countries: The Case of Latin America," mimeo, Kennesaw State College.

Prebisch, R., (1964), *The Economic Development of Latin America and its Principal Problems* (Cambridge: Harvard University Press).

Ram, R., (1985), "Exports and Economic Growth: Some Additional Evidence," *Economic Development and Cultural Change* 33, no. 2: 415–25.

Ram, R., (1987), "Exports and Economic Growth in Developing Countries: Evidence from Time-Series and Cross-Sectional Data," *Economic Development and Cultural Change* 36: 51–72.

Rana, P. R., (1988), "Shifting Revealed Comparative Advantage: Experiences of Asian and Pacific Developing Countries," mimeo, Asian Development Bank, November.

Rhee, Y. W., Ross-Larson, B., and Pursell, G., (1984), *Korea's Competitive Edge* (Washington D.C.: World Bank Research Publication).

Robson, P., (1993), "The New Regionalism and Developing Countries," *Journal of Common Market Studies* 31, no. 3: 329–48.

St. Cyr, E., (1981), "Wages, Prices and the Balance of Payments: Trinidad-Tobago, 1956–74." *Social and Economic Studies*, (September).

Tyler, W. G., (1981), "Growth and Export Expansion in Developing Countries," *Journal of Development Economics* 9 (August): 121–30.

Tyszynski, H., (1951), "World Trade in Manufactured Commodities, 1899–1950," Manchester School of Economic and Social Studies.

United Nations, (1970, 1974, 1978, 1982, 1986, 1988, and 1989), *U.N. Commodity Trade Statistics* (New York: UN Publications).

United Nations, (1970, 1975, 1978, 1982, 1986, 1988, and 1989), *U.N. Yearbook of International Trade Statistics* (New York: UN Publications).

United Nations Conference on Trade and Development (UNCTAD), (1989), "Trade and Development Report," (Geneva: United Nations).

United Nations Industrial Development Organization (UNIDO), (1982), *Changing Patterns of Trade in World Industry: An Empirical Study on Revealed Comparative Advantage* (New York: United Nations, Geneva).

Wade, R., (1988), "The Rise of East Asian Trading Systems—How They Managed Their Trade." Trade Policy Division, World Bank, Washington, D.C.

Watkins, M. H., (1963), "A Staple Theory of Economic Growth," *Canadian Journal of Economic and Political Science* 29.

West Indian Commission, (1992), *Time for Action*, (Wildey, Barbados: Cole's Printery Ltd.).

World Bank, (1991), *World Development Report* (Washington D.C.: World Bank Publications).

World Bank, (1988), "Caribbean Exports: Preferential Markets and Performance," (Washington D.C.: World Bank Publications).

World Bank, (1990a), *World Tables* (1989–1990 edition), (Washington D.C.: World Bank Publications).

World Bank, (1990b), *The Caribbean Common Market Trade Policies and Regional Integration in the 1990's*, Monograph, Trade, Finance and Industry Division, World Bank, Washington, D.C.

Worrell, D., (1987), *Small Island Economies* (New York: Praeger).

Worrell, D., (1989), "Economic Prospects and Policies in Caribbean Economies," mimeo, Research Department, Central Bank of Barbados.

Worrell, D., (1990), "Investment in the Caribbean," mimeo, Research Department, Central Bank of Barbados.

Worrell, D., (1994), "CARICOM: The Integration Experience," mimeo, Research Department, Central Bank of Barbados.

Yang, Y., (1981), "A Comparative Analysis of the Determinants of Non-traditional Exports for Brazil, Israel and South Korea," *Weltwirtsclafthiches Archiv,* Band 117, Heft 3: 497–513.

Yeats, A. J., (1979), "The Changing Pattern of Comparative Advantage in Manufactured Goods." *The Review of Economics and Statistics* 61: 259–66.

Yeats, A. J., (1985), "On the Appropriate Interpretation of the Revealed Comparative Advantage Index," *Weltwirtschaftliches Archiv,* Band, Heft: 61–73.

Yung Whee Rhee, (1985), "Instruments for Export Policy and Administration," World Bank Staff Working Papers no. 725, Washington, D.C.

Yung Whee Rhee, (1989), "Trade Financing For Developing Economies," draft, Industry Development Division, World Bank, Washington, D.C.

Zellner, A., (1962), "An Efficient Method of Estimating Seemingly Unrelated Regressions and Tests for Aggregation Bias," *Journal of American Statistical Association* 57: 585–612.

Zilberfarb, B., (1980), "Domestic Demand Pressure, Relative Prices and the Export Supply Equation—More Empirical Evidence," *Economica* 47, no. 188: 433–513.

# Index

**About the Author**

ARNOLD MEREDITH McINTYRE is an active researcher on trade and development policy issues in the CARICOM region. Recently, he was a country economist at the Caribbean Development Bank and presently, holds the position of Chief (Trade & Economic Policy) at the Economic Affairs Secretariat of the Organization of Eastern Caribbean States.

ISBN 0-275-94745-9

90000>

HARDCOVER BAR CODE

## DATE DUE

| | | | |
|---|---|---|---|
| | | DEC 0 5 2000 | |
| JUNE 5 1996 | | | |
| OCT 1 5 1996 | | | |
| NOV 2 6 1996 | | | |
| APR 0 6 1997 | | | |
| MAY 1 8 1997 | | | |
| DEC 0 1 1997 | | | |
| | | | |
| NOV 1 9 1998 | | | |
| | | | |
| OCT 1 5 2007 | | | |
| | | Printed in USA | |

HIGHSMITH #45230